SHROPS
AND THE NORTH WELSH BORDERS
WALKS FOR MOTORISTS

James F. Edwards

★

30 Walks with sketch maps

COUNTRYSIDE BOOKS
NEWBURY, BERKSHIRE

*Countryside Books' walking guides cover most areas of England and Wales
and include the following series:*

*County Rambles
Walks For Motorists
Exploring Long Distance Paths
Literary Walks*

A complete list is available from the publishers.

First published 1983
by Frederick Warne Ltd.
© James F. Edwards

This completely revised and updated edition
published 1991
© James F. Edwards 1991

COUNTRYSIDE BOOKS
3 Catherine Road
Newbury, Berkshire

ISBN 1 85306 114 X

Sketch maps by the author

Cover photograph taken from Long Mynd above Church Stretton
(Swift Picture Library Ltd.)

PUBLISHERS' NOTE
At the time of publication all footpaths used in these walks were designated
as official footpaths or rights of way, but it should be borne in mind that
diversion orders may be made from time to time.
Although every care has been taken in the preparation of this Guide,
neither the Author nor the Publisher can accept responsibility for those who
stray from the Rights of Way.

Produced through MRM Associates Ltd., Reading
Printed by J. W. Arrowsmith Ltd., Bristol
Typeset by Acorn Bookwork, Salisbury

This book is dedicated to the memory of Jim Taylor who, like many others, is sadly missed.

Acknowledgements

Throughout the survey for this book I have been accompanied by my mother and Jackie Ridgeway. Both are excellent walking companions, having a discerning eye which brought to my attention many things I would otherwise have missed. For their companionship, helpful comments and suggestions, I am most grateful.

Thanks are also due to the staff of the Shropshire Leisure Services, Shrewsbury, and in particular Debbie Hughes for her helpful advice and invaluable assistance with route checking.

Contents

21 ● Vale of Llangollen

1 ● Whitchurch

The Ceiriog Valley ● 22

2 ● Ightfield

Market Drayton ● 4

Selattyn Hill ● 23

Cole Mere ● 3

24 ● Race Course Hill

5 ● Lee Brockhurst

6 ● Clive & Grinshill

Offa's Dyke Path

7 ● Melverley

8 ● SHREWSBURY

9 ● Charlton Hill

Long Mountain ● 25

10 ● Ironbridge
11 ● Ryton

Leighton Park ● 26

12 ● Kenley

Montgomery ● 27

13 ● Worfield

Edenhope Hill ● 28

14 ● Bishop's Castle

15 ● Munslow

Hampton ● 16

17 ● Stokesay

19 ● Bromfield Ludlow
18 ● Cleobury Mortimer
20 ● Whitcliffe Wood

29 & 30 ● Knighton

Introduction

I consider myself to be a very fortunate person. I have good health and a very interesting job which I thoroughly enjoy. But come weekends or holiday time I cannot wait to 'get away from it all' and drive to some interesting location from where I can walk amidst the peace, tranquillity and greenery of the English countryside. To me, this is the very essence of life itself – it is a time to recharge the batteries and forget all about the hurly-burly of our modern high-speed lives, whilst at the same time taking some gentle exercise amongst pleasant surroundings.

The county of Shropshire has an endless variety of rural scenery. The gently rolling agricultural lands of the north; the rich splendour of the South Shropshire Hills; Shrewsbury, sitting proudly within a great loop of the Severn; Ludlow, surely one of England's finest country towns; the dense woodlands of Mortimer Forest; the splendid views from Wenlock Edge; Ironbridge Gorge where modern industry first began; a host of idyllic picturesque villages and lovely country churches just waiting to be explored. The first twenty walks will give you all this, plus many miles of remote country lanes, tracks and paths.

The North Welsh borderland between the Dee Valley and Knighton embraces sixty glorious miles amongst the foothills of the mountains of Wales. It is an area of outstanding natural beauty where every twist and turn exposes fresh scenes of natural splendour.

Twelve hundred years ago, King Offa of Mercia constructed a remarkable earthwork which stretched from the mouth of the Wye to the Dee Valley and passed through this same borderland. Even with the great passage of time since its original construction, Offa's Dyke, as it is now known, is still in a remarkable state of preservation over a considerable length of its route.

In more recent times a long distance footpath has been developed which closely follows the line of this ancient fortification. Sections of this path have been used in the formulation of the last ten walks, thus enabling the walking motorist to observe at first hand part of our national heritage, whilst at the same time enjoying a ramble amidst magnificent scenery.

Shropshire and the North Welsh Borders is an area so rich in natural beauty that I could fill a hundred books with graphic descriptions of every view and landscape. This has not been my intention, as the walkers will see all these things themselves during their jaunts in the countryside. The basic aim has been to ensure that the walking motorist has the confidence to follow an interesting circular route which keeps to the public rights of way.

The walks, which vary in length from 1½ to 9 miles, pass over varied terrain and can be enjoyed by all ages. If you are new to country walking, start with the shorter walks and build up to the longer ones. You will arrive back at the car having enjoyed an excursion into the countryside, feeling refreshed in mind and body.

Rights of Way

All the routes described are on public rights of way, but footpaths can be legally re-routed due to land development or road altera-tions, in which case diversionary signs are usually shown by the Highway Authority.

If a right of way is obstructed, it would be helpful if details of the obstruction, together with its location, are reported to:

> The Rights of Way Officer
> Shropshire County Council
> Winston Churchill Building
> Radbrook Centre
> Radbrook Road
> Shrewsbury, SY3 9BJ

Equipment

Footwear is all important. Waterproof walking shoes or boots are recommended, preferably worn over woollen socks. Smooth soled shoes should not be worn as they can cause accidents and make walking hard work, especially after wet weather.

Lightweight waterproof clothing should always be carried to combat the variable English weather.

A small rucksack can be useful to carry such items as food, cameras, binoculars and the like, which help to make a walk that much more enjoyable.

The Country Code

The Country Code, as follows, makes sound common sense and should be observed at all times:

Enjoy the countryside and respect its life and work
Guard against all risk of fire
Fasten all gates
Keep your dogs under close control
Keep to public paths across farmland
Use gates and stiles to cross fences, hedges and walls
Leave livestock, crops and machinery alone
Take your litter home
Help to keep all water clean
Protect wildlife, plants and trees
Take special care on country roads
Make no unnecessary noise

Shropshire and the North Welsh Borders Walks for Motorists was first published during 1983. Since the original survey was undertaken there have been some changes to the described routes. Therefore a complete new survey has been carried out resulting in a revised and up to date text together with new maps.

So, if you enjoyed the walks in the first edition, choose your ramble, start up the car and prepare to rediscover the delights of Shropshire and its adjacent North Welsh Borderland.

J.F. Edwards
March 1991

A note regarding maps and map references

The Ordnance Survey maps referred to at the beginning of each walk are the 1: 50 000 Landranger Series. Five of these maps cover all the territory of the walks described in this book: maps 117, 126, 127, 137 and 138.

Although you should not encounter problems in finding where to park the car, the text of each walk does contain a grid reference giving the exact parking location.

How to use a grid (map) reference:

If you have never used a map reference before, the reference numbers may seem strange to you, so let's look at an example in order to clarify things:

For Walk 3 (Cole Mere), the map reference given for the parking location is 436 329 on OS map 126. To find this location on the map proceed as follows:

Look along the top, or bottom, of map 126 and find the blue grid number 43. Now estimate a further six tenths of the distance towards grid number 44. This gives point 436, which is the first half of the grid reference.

Now look along the sides of the map and find the blue grid number 32. Now estimate a further nine tenths of the distance towards grid number 33. This gives point 329, which is the second half of the grid reference.

Estimating where imaginary vertical and horizontal lines from these two points cross will give you the parking location on the map.

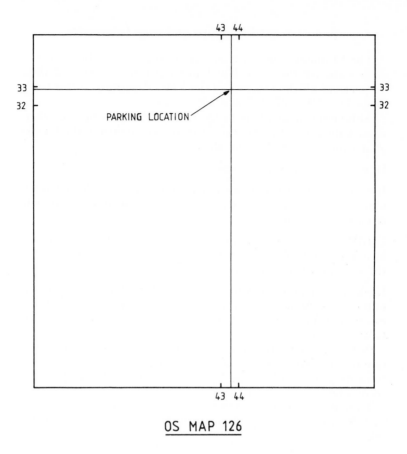

OS MAP 126

In the above example, the parking location is a lane side carpark between the village of Cole Mere and its church, close to the waters of Cole Mere.

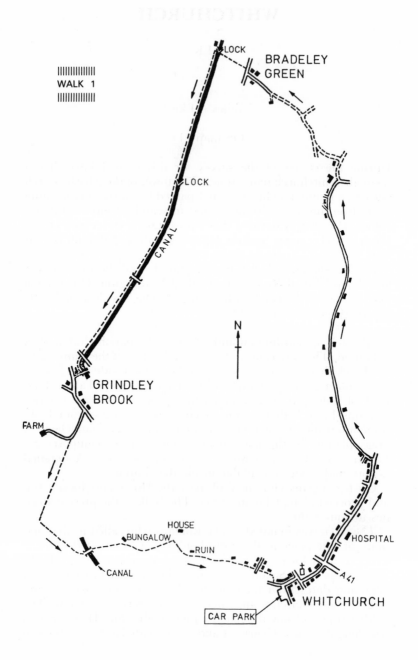

WALK 1

LOCK

BRADELEY
GREEN

LOCK

CANAL

N

GRINDLEY
BROOK

FARM

HOUSE

BUNGALOW

RUIN

HOSPITAL

CANAL

A41

WHITCHURCH

CAR PARK

WHITCHURCH

WALK 1

★

7 miles (11 km)

OS map 117

During the course of the survey for this book I have driven through Whitchurch many times. The tower of the parish church became a familiar sight to me as I passed by on the A41 heading away from my Cheshire homeland in search of more southerly routes. However, I decided that I must take a closer look at this border market town, and the following walk is the result of that visit.

In the shadow of the parish church and headed by the Greyhound Inn there is a road called Yardington. Drive down here and leave the car on a free carpark which is close by Castle Court. (Grid reference: 540 416).

Walk back up Yardington and arrive at the parish church of St Alkmund. The way is now along a road between the church and the Black Bear Inn, but first of all take a look inside the church.

As you enter it a tablet tells why the heart of John Talbot, First Earl of Salop, is buried under the porch. The vast interior contains John Talbot's tomb, a large organ dating from 1756, some interesting stained glass and contemporary chandeliers. A brass plaque by the main door commemorates composer Sir Edward German, who was a native of the town. A detailed history and guide is available inside the church.

On leaving the church, walk past the Horse and Jockey Inn and proceed along Claypit Street. The bulk of the present town lies to your right.

The town was founded by the Romans who called it Mediolanum, or 'the place in the mid plain' as it was situated midway between their fortresses of Chester and Wroxeter (see Walk 9). Then came the Saxons, and the church's dedication to St Alkmund dates from their period. The Normans followed and built a white church from which the town derives its name. The medieval period saw the likes of John Talbot and Henry Percy, who fought against Henry VI and was defeated at Shrewsbury in

13

1403. After the rigours of the Civil War a more peaceful period ensued which produced scholars in place of soldiers.

With the advent of the age of steam the town became an important junction on the railway system, then underwent a complete face-lift when many new dwellings were constructed. World War I saw thousands of troops encamped at nearby Prees Heath and during the second conflict the area became an important bomber airfield. More recent years have seen a gentle industrial expansion on the fringes of the town.

Follow Claypit Street across Brownlow Street. Claypit Street becomes Alport Road which takes you past Whitchurch Hospital, then Church Meadows and Clayton Drive. Turn next left to enter a lane which is headed by signs indicating Wirswall and Hill Valley Golf and Country Club. Pass large detached houses and gently climb along the lane. Continue past Terrick Hall Hotel and the Golf Club. The lane reaches more level terrain and takes you into the County of Cheshire and the scattered hamlet of Wirswall. Gradually climb again, pass Wirswall Farm, and on reaching the top of the climb, turn left to enter a bridleway close by a large dwelling called The Paddocks. The bridleway quickly takes you past a dwelling called The Spinney. Turn left now and follow a track which passes close to an overgrown pond. Continue to a gate which leads onto a winding banked-in track. Turn right and gradually descend along the track – which can be rather boggy after wet weather.

After 300 metres there is a junction where the main track turns to the right. Keep forward here, through a facing gate, and enter an overgrown track hedged in by trees. Emerge onto a short stretch of gravel track which takes you onto a macadam lane some 50 metres to the right of a dwelling. Walk forward and descend along the lane into the tiny hamlet of Bradeley Green. Turn right on reaching the main road, then almost immediately left, to go over a stile where a sign points towards the Sandstone Trail. Follow a field edge to arrive at Willey Moor Lock on the Shropshire Union Canal. Cross the lock and join the canal towpath close by the old lock-keeper's cottage which has been converted into a waterside pub. Turn left and walk along beside the canal, an endless source of fascination with its boats and wildlife.

Follow the towpath for the next 1½ miles and pass an isolated lock and bridge 26 en route. Go under bridge 27 and arrive at Grindley Brook – a well-known haunt of boating enthusiasts. Leave the canalside to the right of bridge 28 where a short stretch of gravel track leads to a crossing road. Turn left and follow the roadside pavement. Pass the Horse and Jockey Inn and a road which goes to Malpas. After 200 metres turn right, cross the road, and enter a farm approach drive over a cattle grid. This farm approach drive commences opposite a small café.

After 250 metres the drive turns to the right and leads to the farm, but keep forward here, across grass, to go over a stile at the side of a facing gate. Walk forward along a field edge, keeping a hedge on your immediate left. After 70 metres go over another stile at the side of a facing field gate and continue along the edge of a very large field, again keeping a hedge on your immediate left. After ¼ mile, and 60 metres before the field corner is reached, go through a gate on the left to enter another large field. Bear diagonally right and after 250 metres cross a double stile at the left side of a field gate. Walk forward now and go over a bridge which crosses the canal.

Walk in the direction of a bungalow which can be seen sitting on a rise straight ahead. Go over a stile in a crossing hedge some 60 metres in front of the bungalow and bear right to shortly pass over another stile at the end of a crossing hedgerow. When I passed this way the route was waymarked by yellow arrows. Climb diagonally to the right, aiming to the right of a detached house which can be seen sitting on a rise straight ahead, and go over a stile and plank-bridge. Climb over a rise in the field then cross a stile at the left of a field gate. The path takes you to the right of a ruinous outbuilding.

The tall square tower of Whitchurch parish church can be seen straight ahead and this is your guide point for the remainder of this waymarked path.

The path gradually descends and takes you over stiles then past the rear of a bungalow. Further stiles take you into a valley which gradually narrows as you approach the town. An overgrown path leads past the rear of dwellings then across the end of a cul-de-sac of new property. A gravel path brings you to steps which take you onto a crossing road.

Turn left and climb back to the carpark which is 200 metres away on the right.

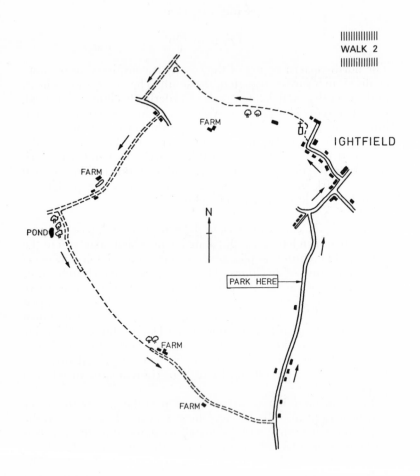

WALK 2

FARM

FARM

POND

IGHTFIELD

N

PARK HERE

FARM

FARM

IGHTFIELD

WALK 2

★

4 miles (6.5 km)

OS map 126

The north-eastern corner of the county is considered to be more civilised, in a rural sense, than the south. The villages are a neat, and generally well kept, array of orderly dwellings. Ightfield, with its remote church, is so typical of an area where a common interest in the land binds together a tight-knit community.

From the cross of the war memorial, in the centre of the village, drive in the direction of Whitchurch (4½) and Ash (2¾). After only 100 metres turn next left and drive down a lane for 350 metres. Park on the right here, where good verge parking is available. (Grid reference: 592 380).

On leaving the car, walk back to the war memorial, pass the post office, then turn left and walk along a lane which takes you to the church. The church is pleasantly situated on a knoll and over-looks a mixture of dwellings. The gargoyles on the church tower have stared out across the surrounding countryside for over five hundred years. Enter the church confines through a gate topped by wrought iron and a hanging lamp. The church is well known for two exceptional brasses: one shows Dame Margery Calveley and dates from 1509, whilst the other is a portrait of her father William Maynwaring. Unfortunately, when I passed this way the building was locked and I had to be content with an external inspection.

From the church entrance continue past the base of the tower and bear right to walk through the graveyard. Pass between the headstones of France and Arkinstall to arrive at a stile which is half hidden in a large hedgerow. Cross the stile and enter a large field. Walk forward, keeping a hedge on your immediate left. The hedge turns to the left shortly and goes towards buildings, but keep forward and walk straight across the field to go through a gate in a crossing hedge. There is a hedge intermingled with oak trees on the left now.

Bear right and walk across the higher ground to pass between

17

telegraph poles. Arrive at a stile which is set in a crossing hedge 10 metres to the left of a field gate and 80 metres to the left of a concrete tank installation. Cross this double stile and plank bridge then continue along a field edge, keeping a fence and hedgerow on your immediate right.

There are long views to the left here, across the agricultural fields of north-east Shropshire.

Pass a concrete triangulation pillar and arrive at a farm approach drive. Turn left and descend to a crossing lane via a cattle grid. Turn left and after 100 metres arrive at a pair of small single-storey lodge-type dwellings on the right which straddle the approach lane to Lea Hall. Pass between these dwellings and walk along the lane. The hall, pleasantly situated at the far side of a man-made pond, comes into view. Walk forward and pass between two large barns via gates. Enter a facing track through another gate.

After 300 metres arrive at a junction of tracks. Turn sharp left here at a facing gate and follow a track through trees. There are sunken ponds in the trees on the right now. A facing gate gives access to a very large field. Walk along the field edge keeping a hedgerow on your immediate left.

Over to the left, Ightfield Church comes into view across the fields.

At the field corner go through a facing gate and follow a track in the direction of a farm which can be seen at the rear of trees straight ahead. The track takes you to the right of the trees and leads to the farm. Go through gates and walk by the farm outbuildings, then pass to the right of the farmhouse to continue along the farm approach drive. After ¼ mile pass by Springs Farm. A further ¼ mile takes you onto a crossing lane where the way is left.

Follow this lane for ¾ mile, to arrive back at the car.

COLE MERE

WALK 3

4 miles (6.5 km)

OS map 126

Shropshire's lake country is contained within the triangle formed by Ellesmere, Welshampton and Cockshutt. There are seven lakes, or meres, in all, the largest being that alongside the A495 road at Ellesmere; but at the centre of things are the secluded waters of Cole Mere where the student of nature will find total satisfaction.

The A528 road links Ellesmere with Cockshutt, Myddle and Shrewsbury. The village of Colemere is less than a mile to the east of the A528 and 2½ miles from Ellesmere. Between the village and its rather isolated church – which is situated on a lane which goes to Lyneal – there is a lane-side carpark overlooking the placid waters of Cole Mere. (Grid reference: 436 329).

Follow the lane which takes you away from the carpark and past the church. A straight ½ mile brings you to a T-junction opposite Lyneal Parish Hall (the old village school). Turn right, and then next left, where a sign says 'Welshampton 1½'. Leave the village behind and after ½ mile follow the lane over the Shropshire Union Canal. A further ¼ mile brings you to a footpath which crosses the lane immediately after passing Lyneal Lodge, which is on the left. Go over a stile on the left here, and walk along a field edge, keeping a fence and trees on your immediate left.

At the field corner cross another stile to enter a large undulating field. Walk foward now, in the same general direction as before, and after 150 metres climb up a facing grassy bank to pass through a gap in a crossing hedge at the right-hand side of an oak tree. Continue in the same general direction and dip, then climb over the brow of a hill before passing through a gap in a crossing hedgerow. Walk across the next field in the same direction as before and pass through another gap in a crossing hedgerow. Keep in the same direction and gradually descend, to almost converge with trees on the left, then go over a stile which is set in a hedge near the bottom of the descent. Cross a small

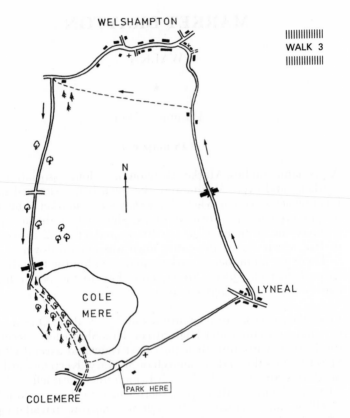

WELSHAMPTON

N

COLE
MERE

LYNEAL

PARK HERE

COLEMERE

rough field and after 100 metres go over a stile at the side of a field gate to enter a lane at its junction with a road.

Turn left and walk along the lane, a pleasant narrow way which takes you through undulating grasslands and affords long views across to the Welsh hills. Go straight over a crossing lane and shortly pass over the canal via a small bridge. There is a renovated thatched black and white cottage on the right now. After a further 50 metres leave the lane to the left and go through a kissing gate to enter Boathouse Wood. Follow a well defined path through trees on level terrain beside the edge of Cole Mere, glimpses of which can be seen through the trees on the left. After ½ mile emerge from the trees and go through a gate and on past the clubhouse of Cole Mere Sailing Club. Pass to the right of a fenced-in boat storage area.

Bear right and walk across open land to arrive back at the carpark.

MARKET DRAYTON

WALK 4

★

4½ miles (7 km)

OS map 127

As its name implies, Market Drayton has a long association with markets, and every Wednesday the town is transformed into a bustling sea of colour when the weekly street market is held. Its origins go back to Norman times, since when the town has survived the torments of the Civil War, and a near disastrous fire in 1651 when almost the entire town was burned down.

There are a number of parking places within the town but the carpark just off Queen Street, and close to the post office, is convenient. (Grid reference: 675 343).

From the carpark entrance turn left and walk along Queen Street to emerge into the wider High Street. Pass Shropshire Street and the Corbet Arms Inn, then turn next right and ascend Church Street to pass the find old church of St Mary. Keep forward past St Mary's Street and the British Legion, then turn left and walk past the vicarage. After a few metres turn next right close by a dwelling called 'Hillside', and follow a narrow macadam path which gradually descends and leads to Walkmill Road.

Turn right and follow the roadside footpath. After ¼ mile turn left opposite Kilnbank Road, then go over a bridge which traverses the river Tern. Keep left, cross a smaller bridge, then quickly turn next left to enter a track. Pass derelict houses and follow the track as it turns to the right close by a bungalow.

Gently climb along the facing track for ¾ mile, passing a pair of isolated dwellings and a farm approach track en route. The track becomes a macadam lane shortly after passing a tiny cottage. Ignore a facing track and follow the lane as it turns to the left. A straight ½ mile leads to a crossing road close to The Four Alls Hotel. Go straight across the road and enter a facing lane in the direction of Tyrley Locks. This pleasant lane passes by the rather plain building of Tyrley church and leads to the Shropshire Union Canal. Go over a stile on the right, just before the bridge, then turn left along the towpath and walk under the

21

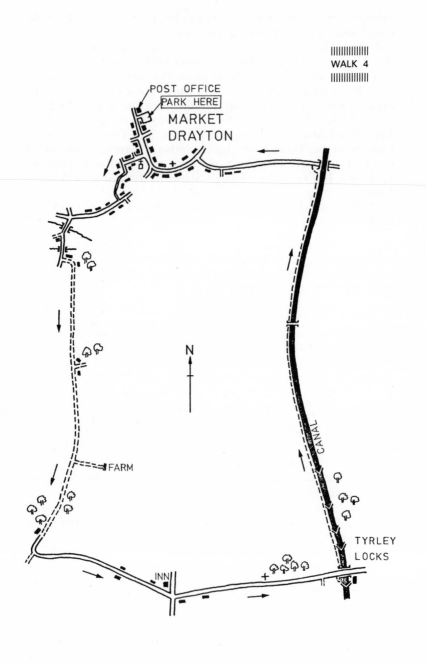

WALK 4

POST OFFICE

PARK HERE

MARKET
DRAYTON

N

FARM

CANAL

TYRLEY
LOCKS

INN

bridge. A rewarding five minutes can be spent here watching the canal boats as they negotiate the locks.

Follow the canal towpath past a series of locks, continue through a rock cutting and pass under bridge No. 61. The canal is now on a raised embankment above the surrounding countryside. Keep an eye open for a lane which passes underneath the canal. Leave the canal towpath here, descend a long flight of stone steps to the lane and follow it away from the canal. Pass Berrisford Close and continue to a T-junction. Turn left, pass the Church of St Thomas of Aquin and a charming mixture of cottages, to arrive at a junction. Turn right and walk past the Red Lion Inn to arrive at High Street in the centre of Market Drayton.

Walk forward now and enter Queen Street which takes you back to the carpark.

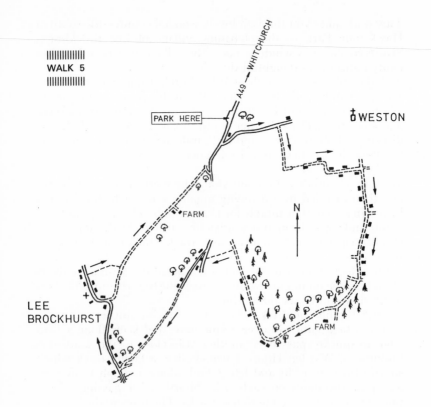

PARK HERE

A49 → WHITCHURCH

☖ WESTON

N

FARM

LEE
BROCKHURST

FARM

LEE BROCKHURST

WALK 5

★

4¾ miles (7.5 km)

OS map 126

This walk takes you through lovely wooded countryside south of Hawkstone Park to the charming village of Lee Brockhurst. Scattered along a winding lane, the village boasts a Norman church and many delightful dwellings.

Eight miles to the south of Whitchurch a minor road crosses the A49 trunk road. The easterly leg of this minor road goes to Weston, Hodnet and Hawkstone Park; the westerly leg to Wem and Ellesmere. Drive further south along the A49 road (in the direction of Shrewsbury) and in ½ mile arrive at a roadside lay-by. Park the car here. (Grid reference: 557 287).

Walk in a southerly direction along the roadside for 200 metres and then turn left by a dwelling to enter a lane which is headed by a sign saying 'Unsuitable for heavy goods vehicles'. Gradually climb and pass through a sandstone cutting. At the top of the climb turn right and enter a grassy track which is hedged in on both sides.

Over to the left can be seen the village of Weston, with its church tower dominant, whilst to its right the tree-topped crags of Elysian Hill break the skyline.

After ¼ mile the track turns left at a facing thicket and takes you to a field gate. Go over a stile here, and keep along a field edge to quickly pass over another stile close to the sandstone building of Warden House Farm. Follow a facing track which shortly turns to right and left. Climb along a rough track now and pass dwellings on each side. Shortly after passing a telephone box arrive at a junction of tracks. The track to the left goes to the village of Weston (½ mile away and well worth the detour) but the way is now right to continue along a level track which takes you past dwellings. Pass numbers 6, 5, 4 and 3 and keep forward past the splendid Rock Cottage (a 'private' sign here refers to vehicular traffic only). Continue past a dwelling called The Woodlands.

Navigational care is now required. There is a private track

which turns to the right, but walk forward between trees and enter a sunken track which descends through a rock cutting. An interesting mix of trees, ferns and woodland plants grow in this area.

Keep to the right where the track forks and proceed along the woodland edge. There is a farm 100 metres away in a field on your left now. The track takes you close by isolated dwellings on your left. Continue along a straight, well-defined track with fields on the left and wooded hills on the right.

Pass a ruinous cottage, then, on passing the next dwelling, keep an eye open for a stile in the fence on the left. Cross the stile and walk over a field in the direction of a bungalow which can be seen straight ahead. A stile and steps take you onto a road opposite the bungalow. Cross the road, turn right, then follow the roadside verge for 80 metres to arrive at a lane which goes off to the left. Enter this lane. The lane takes you past a sawmill and after ¼ mile becomes a grassy track at the left-hand side of a dwelling.

The next ½ mile is along an undulating track which takes you past a couple of isolated dwellings, before descending through a rock cutting to arrive at a crossing lane at the side of a three storey dwelling. An obelisk close by was erected by local tenants as a token of esteem to their landlord, Sir Andrew Vincent Corbet. On the left is a bridge over the river Roden, but turn right and climb along the lane.

You are now entering the scattered village of Lee Brockhurst. The lane turns to the left and takes you to the church, the nave of which was built by the Normans. There is an old studded door and a fine Jacobean communion table.

Continue, pass under telephone wires, then go through a field gate on the right; this gate is almost opposite the entrance drive to a dwelling called The Willows. Climb up a facing field to follow a line of telegraph poles. Go over a stile in a crossing fence and then bear right to pass through a field gate which takes you onto a rough lane. Turn left and gradually climb along the lane.

There are long views to the left shortly and you should be able to pick out the church tower of Wem, 2½ miles away.

Follow the lane for the next ½ mile and arrive close by a bungalow. Enter a facing grassy track here. Continue, and on passing the entrance to a field on the left the track becomes more overgrown. The track descends through trees and leads to a macadam lane. Turn right and climb for a short distance to arrive at a crossing road.

Turn left and follow the roadside verge which leads back to the parking area and the car.

CLIVE AND GRINSHILL

WALK 6

★

3 miles (5 km)

OS map 126

Grinshill Hill is a wooded outcrop of rock seven miles to the north of Shrewsbury. Two interesting villages, Clive and Grinshill, are situated on its lower slopes and are visited during today's short walk. The energetic walker will have a chance to climb to the hilltop, where the effort of climbing is rewarded by magnificent views across the Shropshire Plain, but the more sedate walker will be happy just to circumnavigate the hill by way of tracks and lanes.

The village of Preston Brockhurst lies on the A49 road eight miles from Shrewsbury. Drive away from the A49 in the direction of Clive, Yorton and Myddle and after ½ mile turn left and drive for a further ½ mile to arrive at a carpark set amongst the trees of Corbet Wood. (Grid reference: 525 238).

Walk out of the carpark and turn left to follow a track which is headed by a sign saying 'Vehicular Access to Frontages Only'. (A deep, disused quarry is over the wall on the left.) Pass cottages on right and left. There is a path to the left now – just before a dwelling on the right is reached – which climbs to the summit of Grinshill Hill, 400 metres away. The views from the top of the hill are very rewarding and if the day is clear you should see the Breidden Hills to the south-west and The Long Mynd to the south of Shrewsbury.

Retrace your route back to the track and continue. The spire of Clive church comes into view shortly. The track goes over exposed slabs of rock and takes you past the primary school, before descending to a crossing lane close by the church. Turn right and then left, to follow a lane where there is a row of tall Scotch pines on the right. The lane takes you past dwellings old and new. Turn next left and walk past Clive Methodist Church.

This compact village is an interesting blend of the old intermingled with the new and is a place where well-tended gardens complement each other, presenting an appealing picture to the discerning eye.

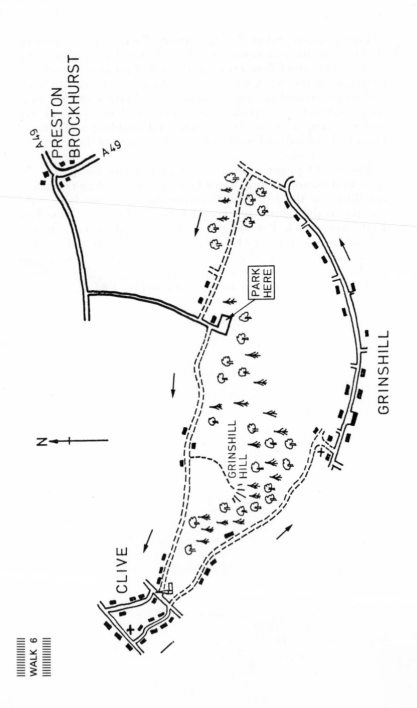

PRESTON
BROCKHURST

A49

A49

N

PARK HERE

GRINSHILL

GRINSHILL HILL

CLIVE

WALK 6

Turn next left and gradually climb up Back Lane. On passing the vicarage, the lane bends sharply to the left. Go straight over a crossing lane and follow a track at the side of the church confines. Continue on this track for ½ mile as it takes you past dwellings and winds around the afforested outcrop of Grinshill Hill. Bear to the right where a circular seat is set at the base of an oak tree and continue past the small, delightful building of Grinshill church. Turn left and walk through the centre of the attractive village of Grinshill.

Pass the Elephant and Castle Inn and, a little further on, the delightful manor house of Stone Grange. There are more modern dwellings on the left now. Continue to where the lane turns sharply to the right – but keep left here, where a narrow lane leads into a track. Pass between tall, tree-lined banks then keep left where the track forks. The track climbs through a rock cutting. Pass a track which goes off to the right, then walk past dwellings and turn left at a T-junction.

A straight walk of 200 metres takes you back to the carpark.

MELVERLEY

WALK 7

★

3¾ miles (6 km)

OS map 126

The village of Crew Green, 11 miles to the west of Shrewsbury, straddles the B4393 road midway between the A458 and A483 roads. Drive down a lane close by the Fir Tree Inn where a sign tells you that Melverley is one mile away. After ¼ mile, drive over a long narrow bridge which takes you over the river Severn and leave the car on a parking area at the right-hand side of the road. (Grid reference: 331 158).

Cross the lane and go over a fence-stile set in a hedgerow. Bear right and follow a well-defined footpath along the top of an earth floodbank. Floodbanks like this are a feature of the area and were built in an early attempt to contain the flood waters of the Severn and Vyrnwy.

Pass over three fence-stiles. On the left now is the winding river Vyrnwy which merges with the Severn just upstream from the bridge close to where the car is parked. Walk across a facing field bearing very slightly to the left. Go over a stile at the field corner and continue along a riverside path between hedges. Pass close to outbuildings then enter the confines of Melverley church.

The church, which was built during the reign of Henry IV, is most impressive. A true black and white gem, it was constructed from massive oak timbers, resulting in an overall appearance of rugged simplicity. There is much to interest the inquiring visitor – sturdy oak benches, a fine Jacobean pulpit, an ancient font and a narrow twisting stairway which gives access to a most unusual gallery.

A small gate at the rear of the church gives access to a path which again follows the top of an earth floodbank close to the river. Pass over three stiles and continue past a farm which can be seen on the opposite side of the river. There is an impressive view of Breidden Hill and Rodney's Pillar over to the left. The Vyrnwy forms the border with Wales and if the day is clear the Welsh Mountains can be seen straight ahead. Go over two more stiles and pass a dwelling on the other side of the river.

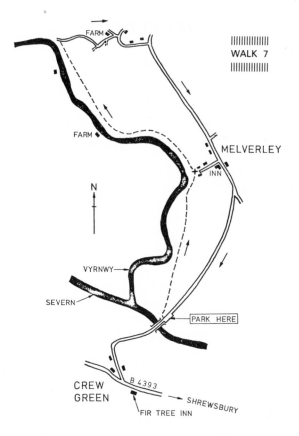

A further stile gives access to a narrow lane. The river turns away to the left here, but turn sharp right and follow the lane which quickly becomes a rough track between hedgerows. After 150 metres follow the main track as it bends to the left. Keep forward to a crossing lane. There is a farm on the left here, but turn right and then immediately right again to follow a lane which takes you, after 500 metres, to a T-junction. Turn right. A straight ½ mile takes you into Melverley. Pass a lane on the left which goes to Pentre and Shrewsbury and arrive at the Tontine Hotel.

There are two alternatives now: either continue forward along the lane in the direction of Crew Green and Welshpool, a gentle ½ mile taking you back to the bridge across the Severn and the carpark; or turn right and walk up to Melverley church and then retrace your original route back to the car.

31

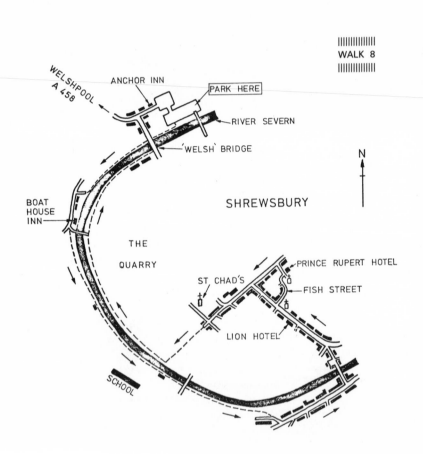

WALK 8

WELSHPOOL A 458

ANCHOR INN

PARK HERE

RIVER SEVERN

'WELSH' BRIDGE

SHREWSBURY

N

BOAT HOUSE INN

THE

QUARRY

ST CHAD'S

PRINCE RUPERT HOTEL

FISH STREET

LION HOTEL

SCHOOL

SHREWSBURY

WALK 8

★

2¾ miles (4.5 km)

OS map 126

It was a clear blue autumn day when I first explored the winding streets and narrow ways of Shrewsbury. I strolled where every view and vista echoed the wonderful weather and made me feel totally at peace with the world. The initial stroll alongside the Severn, the historical charm of old timber buildings, the graceful lines of towers and spires, half-hidden views down cobbled alleyways and a lovely waterside park – all are indelibly etched on my memory.

From the town centre, drive along the A458 in the direction of Welshpool and cross the Severn via a stone bridge which is aptly named 'Welsh Bridge'. (As you cross this bridge you will see a large pedestrian footbridge also crossing the river on your right.) Immediately after crossing Welsh Bridge turn right, pass the Anchor Inn and leave the car on the large Frankwell carpark. There is a modest fee to pay here. (Grid reference: 489 128).

Walk to the riverside and turn right to follow a path which takes you through a narrow arch underneath Welsh Bridge and make your way along the riverside promenade for 300 metres. The way is now right to join a crossing road. Turn left and follow a roadside pavement to the Boat House Inn. This pleasant hostelry, with its colourful signboards depicting various watery scenes, is at the site of an old ferry crossing. The ferry has been replaced by a narrow suspension bridge which enables pedestrians to cross the river at this point.

Rejoin the riverside and follow a macadam path, which takes you away from the Boat House Inn and the footbridge, and pass in front of a large boathouse. The building at the top of the slope on your right is part of the famous Shrewsbury School.

On the other side of the river, and overlooking a gently sloping waterside park, can be seen the domed church of St Chad.

Pass in front of the school boathouse and walk under a crossing bridge. The path takes you over a crossing stream via a tiny bridge, then gradually climbs away from the riverside to merge with an avenue leading to a crossing road. Turn left and walk along the roadside pavement, pass an intermix of dwellings and shops then turn left at the chemist's. Walk over a narrow bridge across the Severn, pass the Acorn Inn and continue past the head of Beeches Lane to turn left into Wyle Cop. Climb past shops displaying many varied wares in this area which contains a host of interesting buildings.

A narrative on the Henry Tudor House tells that King Henry VII lodged here prior to the Battle of Bosworth Field in August 1485. Take a peep along an interesting narrow courtyard which commences under this building. A little further on from the Henry Tudor House is the Lion Hotel. Continue, and on passing St Julian's Church, turn right and ascend the narrow Fish Street.

Shrewsbury is rich in old houses and there are many fine examples in this area, mostly black and white, dating from the fifteenth, sixteenth and seventeenth centuries. The delightful Three Fishes Inn faces St Alkmund's Church, whilst close by is a house where John Wesley preached his first sermon in Shrewsbury.

Follow the cobbles and bear right to arrive opposite the Prince Rupert Hotel. Turn left and walk past the Abbot's House and the Bull Inn. Turn next left and enter the modern shopping centre of Shrewsbury; walk past High Street, then Market Street, and keep forward to enter St John's Hill which commences at the left of the Exchange Hotel. Pass Cross Hill to arrive at St Chad's Terrace. The way is now forward into Quarry Place, but first of all have a look at St Chad's Church, a short walk to your right.

The church, one of England's few classical round churches, was rebuilt in 1790 after the previous building had collapsed. There are numerous items of interest over which to ponder.

Go through wrought iron gates at the end of Quarry Place and enter 'The Quarry' — a gentle parkland leading down to the Severn. The park is so named because much of the red stone to be seen in the town was quarried from this area after which it was landscaped to good effect.

Walk to the riverside, turn right and go past the pedestrian bridge which leads to the Boat House Inn. On leaving the park, follow a roadside pavement that takes you back to Welsh Bridge. Cross it and walk back to the carpark.

CHARLTON HILL

WALK 9

★

4¾ miles (7.5 km)

OS map 126

Five miles to the south-east of Shrewsbury, and just off the B4380 road close to its intersection with the A5, is the site of the fourth city of Roman Britain. Known to us as Wroxeter, its Roman name was Viroconium. The area is being thoroughly excavated and a visit to this interesting site makes a pleasant prelude to today's walk.

From the Roman remains, drive along the B4380 road in the direction of Buildwas and Ironbridge, pass a lane which leads to Donnington and Charlton Hill, and arrive at a crossroads two miles from Wroxeter. The road to the right goes to Dryton and Eyton and that to the left leads to Longwood and Wellington, but drive 250 metres further on and leave the car at the side of the B4380 road where there is adequate verge parking available. (Grid reference: 589 063).

On leaving the car, go forward along the roadside, pass over the brow of a hill then immediately turn left to pass through a small wooden gate which gives access to a field. This gate is about 200 metres from where the car is parked. Walk across the field, bearing slightly right, then continue with a hedge on your left. At the field corner go through a gap then proceed along a track with the hedge now on your right. A fine view of the Wrekin can be enjoyed from here, whilst in the near distance the church of Eaton Constantine comes into view.

The track becomes hedged in and emerges at a lane on the edge of Eaton Constantine village. The way is now left to follow a lane which climbs past the church, but first of all walk forward and have a look at the splendid black and white timber-framed house where Richard Baxter, the seventeenth century author and preacher, spent his boyhood. Follow the lane as it gradually climbs past the church. At the crossroads ahead, keep forward in the direction of Charlton Hill and Donnington. The lane climbs. Near the top of the climb the lane forks; keep left here and walk

35

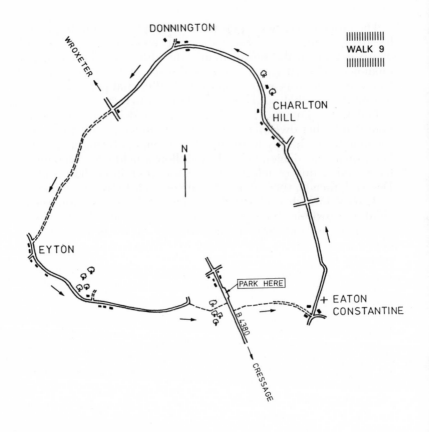

past the once opulent Charlton Hill House. The lane skirts around the side of Charlton Hill and is a platform for extensive views over the surrounding countryside. The spires and towers of Shrewsbury can be seen and, if the day is clear, the far-off mountains of Wales smudge the horizon to the left.

The lane descends then takes you through the tiny hamlet of Donnington. Arrive at a crossing road. Cross the road and go through a facing gate to follow a grassy track along a field edge. A facing gate leads into a large undulating field. Continue, keeping a hedgerow on your immediate right. Pass through another gate and follow a rough track, again keeping a hedgerow on your immediate right. A further gate leads into a hedged-in track which emerges onto a crossing lane close to a farm. Turn left and pass through the tiny village of Eyton-on-Severn.

The unseen river Severn meanders through fields on the right, less than ½ mile away. Also on the right can be seen an old tower which is built in the Elizabethan style, although its origins are unknown. The village was the birthplace of Lord Herbert of Cherbury, who was a philosopher and influential political figure during the first half of the seventeenth century.

Follow the lane as it winds and pass a delightful thatched house and other dwellings. Gradually climb for ⅓ mile to where the lane turns sharply to the left. Go through a facing field gate here, then bear diagonally right to follow a field edge keeping a fence and a line of telegraph poles on your immediate right. Descend, then go through a field gate on your right and immediately pass through a small gate into a wood. Cross a stream, then climb forward for 60 metres to a second gate which leads into a field. Turn left and climb up the field edge. At the field corner go over a fence to arrive on a crossing road close to where the car is parked.

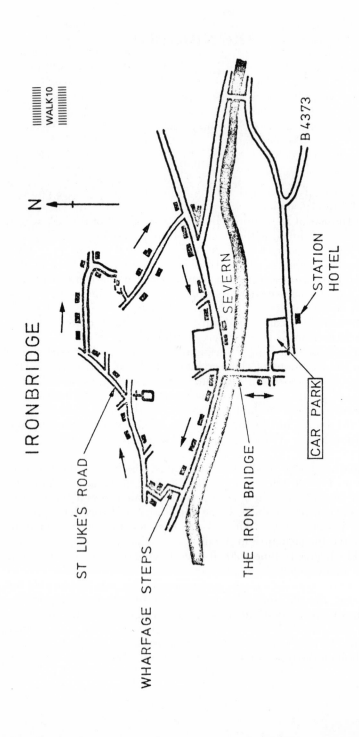

IRONBRIDGE

WALK10

N

ST LUKE'S ROAD

WHARFAGE STEPS

THE IRON BRIDGE

SEVERN

B 4373

STATION HOTEL

CAR PARK

IRONBRIDGE

WALK 10

★

1½ miles (2.5 km)

OS map 127

This walk is a total deviation from the norm. Cross-country paths and rural views are replaced by scenes more reminiscent of the Industrial Revolution. But it is a stroll full of interest where we can well imagine the struggle of the people initially responsible for our modern way of life. We owe a great debt to these early industrial pioneers of the Ironbridge Gorge, for it was in this area, during the eighteenth century, that modern industry first began. During recent years much has been done to preserve a part of our heritage which had fallen into decline, and many interesting workshops and museums bring back to life skills and practices from a bygone age. Coalbrookdale Museum of Iron boasts Abraham Darby's original 1709 furnace, Coalport shows you the traditions of china-making, whilst at nearby Blists Hill there is an open-air museum where the trades of printing, plastering and saw cutting can be observed at close quarters.

Leave the car on the Ironbridge carpark which is situated just off the B4373 on the Broseley side of the Severn, close by the Station Hotel. (Grid reference: 672 033).

Make your way to the famous bridge which gave the town its name. The old toll house has been turned into a tourist information centre where details of a nature trail through the nearby woods can be obtained. Cross the bridge and turn left opposite the Tontine Hotel. This is the best location from which to observe the structure in detail.

The bridge is almost 200 ft long, having one span of 100 ft and two smaller ones. It is believed to be the first iron bridge ever to be built. Abraham Darby of Coalbrookdale was responsible for casting the 380 tons of iron which went into its construction. Almost two years in the making, the bridge was opened to traffic on New Year's Day, 1781. Although it was closed to vehicular traffic in 1934 it remains open to cyclists and pedestrians.

Follow the roadside pavement alongside the Severn. You may

39

be lucky and see one of the few remaining coracle makers testing his craft on this section of the river. Pass the White Hart Inn then turn right to ascend Wharfage Steps. On reaching the top of this narrow twisting climb, turn right and continue. Climb to the left where the ways fork. There is another clear view of the Iron Bridge now, down on the right.

Arrive at a crossing lane close by St Luke's Church. Climb up St Luke's Road and shortly pass a school-like building. The lanes fork – bear left here and continue to climb. Keep next right and continue along level terrain. Turn next right where the lane turns sharply to the right (before No. 10) and descend. After 80 metres the lane becomes a path on passing a dwelling called Winterwood. Follow this path which takes you past the rear of a dwelling whose eaves are at eye level. Walk forward now on to a macadam lane, then turn left at the crossing way ahead. Descend to the main road, turn right and follow the roadside pavement into the town centre.

You may like to survey an interesting assortment of shops in the Town Square before crossing the bridge on your way back to the carpark.

RYTON

WALK 11

★

3¾ miles (6 km)

OS map 127

From Telford the A464 runs in a south-easterly direction and passes through Shifnal on its way to Wolverhampton. On the southern side of Shifnal, close by the hospital, is a minor road which leads to Ryton and Beckbury. Drive along this road for a straight 1½ miles and pass a lodge gate entrance of Evelith Manor, followed by Sands Farm. Park the car ⅓ mile further on where there is a long grass verge on the right. (Grid reference: 753 043).

Walk back to Sands Farm and enter a track on the right which is headed by a sign saying 'To Hatton Grange – Farms Only'. Pass a couple of dwellings. The track becomes a narrow macadam lane which takes you past the splendid three storey farmhouse of Hatton Grange. The route to the farm turns to the left over a cattle grid, but keep forward here and enter a rough track between hedgerows. After ½ mile, the track descends between banks of gorse and bracken and then takes you over a crossing stream. The track turns to the right shortly, then becomes a path which goes up a gully to a facing gate. Go through the gate and walk across a field keeping a fence on your immediate right. The path emerges onto a crossing lane close to dwellings. Turn right and walk up to Ryton church.

The villagers are very proud of their church and this is shown by a notice from the churchwardens which says 'To appreciate to the full our chancel and beautiful east window, we suggest that you turn on the marked switches adjacent to the font'. This approach is most encouraging when access to so many of our lovely country churches is today being denied to visitors. The chancel and east window are indeed a most beautiful sight with the lights on – but please remember to switch them off. Other items of interest include a fourteenth century font and traces of very old stonework in the east and south walls.

Leave the church and descend along a track to arrive at a

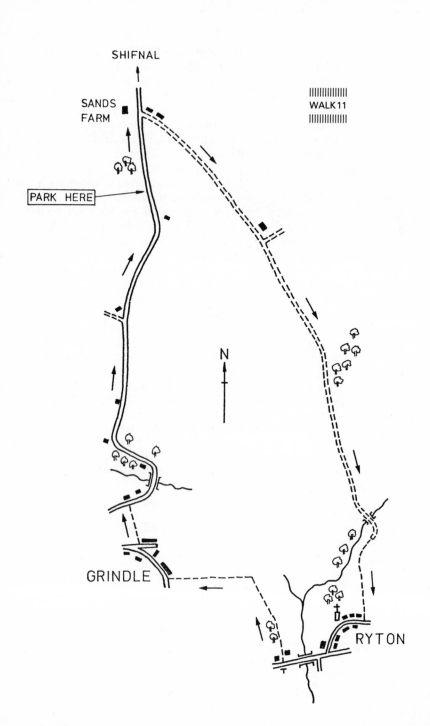

SHIFNAL

SANDS FARM

WALK 11

PARK HERE

N

GRINDLE

RYTON

crossing road. Turn right in the direction of Shifnal and Telford, pass a lane which goes to Beckbury, then go over a bridge which traverses the river Worfe. Leave the road to the right, opposite a telephone kiosk, where a narrow passage takes you between dwellings. Cross a stile in a crossing fence which gives access to a large field. Climb diagonally to the left through scattered trees and, on reaching more level ground, gradually walk closer to a hedge which merges from the left. There is a splendid view of Ryton church now, over to the right, across the valley.

Go over a stile on the left, next to a field gate. Walk along a field edge now, keeping a hedge on your immediate left. A field gate close by a dwelling gives access to a crossing lane in which turn right and walk into the hamlet of Grindle. There is an interesting old cottage on the right shortly. The lane turns to the left now, but enter a narrow path which commences over a stile opposite a telephone kiosk and takes you close by a dwelling. Cross a fence-stile and enter a field.

Keeping a fence on your immediate left, gradually climb, then pass over stiles in a crossing hedge and fence. Descend, and emerge on to a crossing lane via a stile and steps. Turn right and walk past cottages. Cross a long sandstone bridge and once again pass over the Worfe. The lane turns sharply to the left past an outcrop of sandstone rock and shortly turns to the right where there is a rather odd-looking chalet style dwelling on the left. Continue and climb past a three storey cottage, then walk past the entrance drive of Hinnington Grange.

A gentle stroll of ⅓ mile takes you back to the car.

KENLEY

2½ miles (4 km)

OS map 126

Cottage, farm, church and post office; Kenley has all the ingredients of a typical rural village. Sitting proudly upon a ripple in the landscape four miles due west of Much Wenlock, it is the ideal location from which to enjoy superb views along the wooded backbone of Wenlock Edge, while from the tiny churchyard there are long views to the Stretton Hills and Wales.

Park the car on a small triangular-shaped piece of ground at the side of the lane 300 metres south of the church and close to where a track joins the lane. (Grid reference: 562 005).

Walk along the lane to the church, the walls of which are very thick at the base and taper towards a roof that carries 500 year old supporting beams. A tablet set into the walls is dedicated to Archibald Alison, who wrote *Essays on the Nature and Principles of Taste*. The bell tower dates from the thirteenth century and the church contains a fine canopied Jacobean pulpit and a tiny organ. The view from the base of the bell tower takes in Shrewsbury straight ahead and long views towards Wales over to the left.

From the church continue along the lane. On the right shortly is the recently converted old schoolhouse. Turn next right and walk along a gravel track between hedgerows. A facing gate gives access to a large field. Walk forward with a hedgerow on your immediate right at first, then keep forward where the hedgerow kinks to the right, to shortly pass through a field gate. Over to the right is a small farm. After 80 metres go through another gate, walk forward and gradually descend along a rough gravel track.

There are splendid views from here of Wenlock Edge, dominating the skyline in both directions.

On the left there are large farm outbuildings and a house. Go through a gateway and follow a straight track to a gate which gives access to a crossing lane. Turn right and walk along the lane. After ½ mile keep an eye open for a hedged-in track which

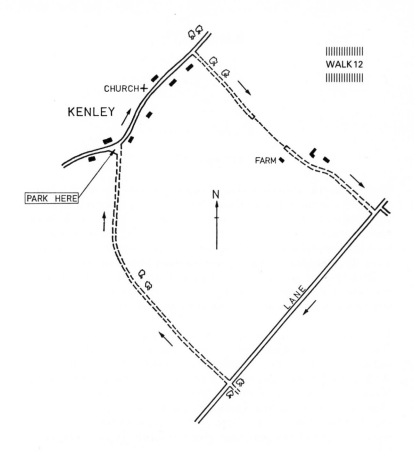

crosses the lane. Leave the lane here, and enter the track on the right, via a gate. Gradually climb, then pass through a crossing gate. Follow a short length of tree-lined path then continue once again along a hedged-in track.

This track takes you back to Kenley and the car.

WORFIELD

WALK 13

★

5 miles (8 km)

OS map 138

The river Worfe meanders peacefully through quiet water-meadows prior to its confluence with the Severn close to Bridgnorth. This is an area which attracted the Normans, and many of their successors are still entrenched on estates held by the same families for centuries. It is an area where gentle wooded hills, scenic riverside views and interesting picturesque villages combine to form an attractive rural landscape.

The A454 road links Bridgnorth with Wolverhampton. Opposite a roadsign which says Bridgnorth 3 and Wolverhampton 10½, there is a roadside carpark. The carpark is also close to the start of a lane which goes to Roughton (½) and Barnsley (1). (Grid reference: 761 946).

Park the car, cross the road and turn right to follow the roadside verge away from Bridgnorth. After 350 metres turn left opposite a black and white cottage to follow a narrow lane between dwellings. Go through a gate to leave the dwellings behind. Shortly, there is a farm on the left, then a facing gate. A footpath commences on your right here, through a kissing gate. Follow this fenced-in footpath as it turns to the right and stays parallel with an adjoining drive. Cross a stream via a footbridge and continue. Emerge from the footpath, then pass between two houses to arrive at a crossing road. Turn left, cross the river, then turn next right by the war memorial. Pass Chestnut Drive and enter the charming village of Worfield.

There are many delightful cottages in the village, and a lot of original timber framing survives from a bygone age. The church stands proudly at the end of a long row of cottages where its spire, almost 200 ft high, dominates the surrounding landscape. The base of the church is over 700 years old, and there is much fine carving to be seen inside. There is fourteenth century glass, and the imposing tomb of Sir Edward Bromley and his wife. Across the lane from the church is a splendid half-timbered hall set in a walled garden.

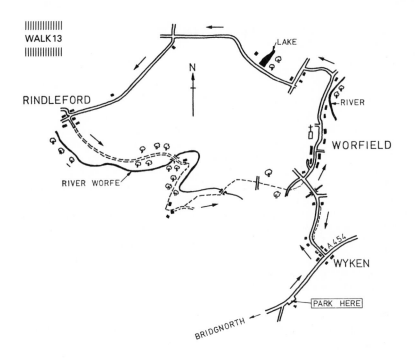

WALK 13

RINDLEFORD

LAKE

RIVER

WORFIELD

RIVER WORFE

WYKEN

PARK HERE

BRIDGNORTH

Continue along the lane and pass a narrow way on the left which is unsuitable for heavy goods vehicles. The lane takes you past isolated dwellings, then between the Worfe and a large sandstone cliff riddled with caves. Turn next left opposite a dwelling called Hallonsford and climb along a rough lane to a crossing road. Turn left, pass a small cemetery, and then turn next right by farm buildings and descend. At the bottom of the hill a broad valley will be seen on the left and a lake on the right, the tranquil haunt of many species of water fowl.

Climb along the facing lane and, after ½ mile, arrive at a crossroads. Turn left and descend for a further ½ mile to arrive at the tiny hamlet of Rindleford. The main lane turns sharply to the right here, but go left through a gate opposite Old Mill Cottage and enter a track between a dwelling on the left and a mill-like outbuilding on the right. Go through a gate which is close to a cottage on the left and follow a macadam way.

There is a grassy bank on the left and a flat narrow field on the right. The way passes close to the Worfe and takes you by two cattle grids before crossing the river via a stout stone bridge. Pass by another cattle grid and walk past the rear of a detached

47

dwelling. Go over a stile at the side of a gate and, keeping on level ground, follow the base of a rock band which bends away to the right.

A path takes you to a stile at the side of a small gate. Cross the stile and continue through trees to climb above the river which is down on your left. Emerge from the trees and walk past the rear of a cottage. Turn left at the end of the cottage garden, cross a stile, and walk to a gate at the left of a large stone outbuilding. The gate gives access to a field. Walk to the right of a line of telegraph poles and converge with a rough farm track, but quickly leave this track to the left and pass under the telephone wires to descend along a grassy track which takes you to a stile in a crossing fence by a gate close to the river. Cross the stile and follow the riverside for 250 metres to arrive at a small footbridge by the remains of an old mill.

Cross the footbridge. Davenport House can be seen on top of higher ground straight ahead. Walk forward aiming to the right of the house and pass through a field gate to climb up a facing gully along a rough sandy track. Climb to the right of a large isolated tree and on reaching level ground walk straight over a crossing macadam drive. The path descends shortly to a crossing macadam drive. Go over a stile here which is set in a facing fence on the other side of the drive. Bear diagonally left now and cross a large field. Cross a stile at the field corner and turn left to quickly pass over a second stile at the side of a gate. You have now entered a lane close to the war memorial on the outskirts of Worfield village. Turn right.

You are now back on part of your original route. Retrace your way back to the A454 road and the car.

BISHOP'S CASTLE

WALK 14

★

3½ miles (5.5 km)

OS map 137

The quaint little town of Bishop's Castle is at the junction of the A488 and B4385 roads. Although there are now only traces of the original castle from which it takes its name, the town has many interesting features and possesses a tiny town hall built on a hill at the top of the town 200 years ago. There is also a fine church and many old buildings which blend with more modern surroundings.

Leave the car on the large carpark off Station Street. (Grid reference: 324 887).

From the carpark entrance turn right and then turn left at the Boars Head Inn to walk along Church Street. There is an interesting row of black and white cottages on the left and the parish church lies at the head of the street. It has a splendid lychgate but unfortunately little remains of the original twelfth century building as the church suffered greatly during the Civil War and was mainly renewed in 1860.

Turn right opposite the church at the Six Bells Inn. Pass a turn-off to the left and continue past the police station. Turn next left down Grange Road. At the end of the road go through a small wooden gate and follow a short stretch of path which takes you past a cottage. Emerge onto a crossing lane in which turn left, then bear right and walk past the modern dwellings of The Ridge. Gradually climb along the lane and pass a track which goes off to the left. The lane descends. At the bottom of the descent is a small bridge over a stream but 30 metres before this bridge is a field gate on the left at the side of a large oak tree; go through this gate and walk forward along a path which never strays too far away from the stream on the right. The path takes you over coarse, but level, terrain. After ¼ mile go over a stile at the side of a large oak tree growing next to the stream.

Cross three fields via a gate and stiles then continue along flat terrain between a hillside on the left and the stream on the right.

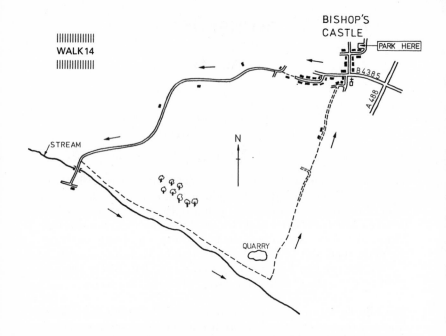

Keep an eye open for the remains of a small quarry set into the hillside on the left. Walk forward past the quarry then turn to the left before reaching a crossing hedge and climb along a rough grassy track. Pass to the left of a fence and hedge which jut out from the field corner, then go over a stile in a crossing hedge 30 metres further on and walk along a field edge keeping a hedgerow on your immediate right. Go through a gateway at the field corner and walk along the edge of another field, again keeping a hedgerow on your immediate right.

A stile at the side of a facing field gate takes you on to a rough grassy track. After passing through another gate the main track turns to the left and climbs, but keep forward and follow a narrow hedged-in path. Go through gates at the side of a dwelling and walk forward along a track where Bishop's Castle comes into view straight ahead. Descend, then turn right at the T-junction. Turn next left and pass the fire station to emerge at a crossing road next to the church.

Enter Church Street at the side of the Six Bells Inn and retrace your original route back to Station Street and the car.

MUNSLOW

WALK 15

★

4 miles (6.5 km)

OS map 138

Towards the southern end of Wenlock Edge there are many delightful hamlets nestling in hidden hollows and vales out of sight of the passing motorist. If you are driving along the B4368 between Much Wenlock and Craven Arms you will pass through Munslow but the real village sits in a hollow out of sight, so leave the main road and drive in the direction of Munslow church.

Park the car just before the church on the left, where there is good verge parking available. (Grid reference: 522 877).

The church fabric is of mixed dates and the styles vary from Norman through to the Victorian era. There is some excellent stained glass and interesting monuments and – surprisingly – a brick from the Great Wall of China!

Walk past the church and enter a bridleway on the right, which commences close to the Coach House. Turn left before a facing gate and climb along a grassy path which soon turns into a rough path up a narrow rocky gully. After 400 metres emerge from this narrow way at a gate which takes you onto a track coming from the left. Keep forward here through a facing gate and gradually climb along the track between banked hedges and ferns. There is a wood shortly on your right. Keep forward past a track which goes off to the left. There are trees on both sides of the track now. At the top of the climb, at a T-junction of tracks, turn right where a broad track takes you along level terrain. An extremely good view of Brown Clee Hill appears shortly, through a clearing in the trees on the right.

The track narrows and then descends and turns to the left through trees. Follow this wooded track for almost ½ mile, then emerge from the trees through a facing gate. The path skirts a field edge and goes towards a farm. Walk close to a fence on your right and then pass a couple of small outbuildings to arrive at the field corner. Go through a facing gate then turn sharp left and gradually climb up a gentle gully.

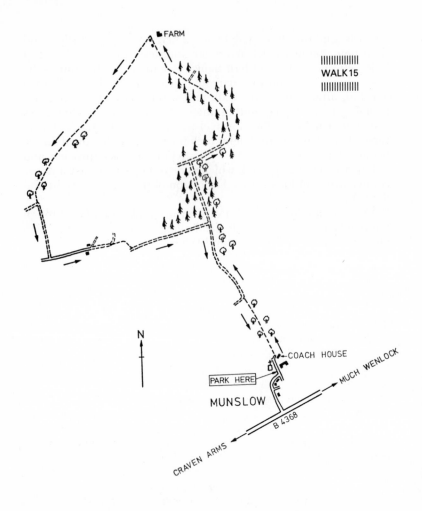

N

FARM

COACH HOUSE

MUCH WENLOCK

PARK HERE

MUNSLOW

CRAVEN ARMS

B 4368

After 60 metres go through a gate and continue up the tree-lined gully until a gate in a crossing fence gives access to a large field. Walk along the field edge and gradually climb, keeping a hedge and fence on your immediate right. A gate at the field corner leads on to a path which follows the edge of a wood on the left. Shortly, down on the right, can be seen the black and white houses of the tiny hamlet of Middlehope.

Near the top of the climb the path cuts through the wood, then emerges from the trees. Fine vistas over Corvedale, and beyond towards Ludlow, now delight us. There are tracks to left and right now; follow the left-hand one and descend for a straight ¼ mile between widely set fern banks. A gate at the bottom of the descent takes you on to a narrow macadam lane in which turn left and, after 300 metres walk past a bungalow. Go through a facing gate and pass outbuildings. Another facing gate gives access to a field. Follow a gravel track. Leave the track shortly through a gate on the right to follow a path hemmed in by hedges, ferns and trees. At a T-junction of ways turn left and follow a wide grassy track which shortly takes you past a dense conifer wood and leads to a T-junction of tracks. Turn right and descend.

You are now back on part of your original route. Go through the two facing gates, then descend along the narrow gully which takes you back to Munslow and the car.

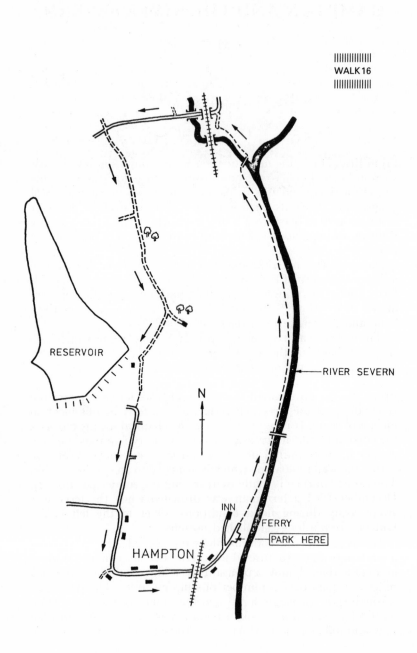

||||||||||||
WALK 16
||||||||||||

RESERVOIR

RIVER SEVERN

N

INN

FERRY

PARK HERE

HAMPTON

HAMPTON AND THE RIVER SEVERN

WALK 16

★

4½ miles (7 km)

OS map 138

From Bridgnorth, the majestic river Severn flows south to Bewdley and beyond. There are no crossing bridges for traffic on this stretch of river, and this helps to maintain an unspoilt area of countryside. The only intrusion into a peaceful stroll by the river is the occasional blast from a steam whistle on the Severn Valley Railway which follows a delightful route never very far from the river.

Hampton is situated on the west bank of the river Severn, five miles to the south of Bridgnorth and three miles from the B4363. Drive under the railway bridge then park on the right, some 50 metres or so before a crossing gate which gives access to the river bank and the ferry. (Grid reference: 746 865).

The walk can also commence from Hampton Loade, which is on the east bank of the river not far from the A442, but this necessitates the use of the ferry in order to cross the river.

From the car go through the gate and walk forward along the riverside, past the ferry. There has been a ferry at this location for many years. It is not powered by mechanical means but uses the current to take it across the river. The ferryman puts the long rudder in the required direction and the ferry moves crabwise across the water via a line which is attached to an overhead wire. The return journey is made by reversing the rudder position. In December 1964 a ferryman was drowned when the ferry was swept away during flood conditions. Over to the left is the Unicorn Inn, a long-established hostelry.

Go over a fence and continue along the riverside, then pass under a modern bridge structure which carries two large diameter pipes across the river. Follow a pleasant riverside path for a further 1½ miles and pass over a number of stiles en route. The path goes through quite dense undergrowth then takes you across a stout footbridge over Mor Brook, a tributary of the Severn. Turn left now and follow a path which skirts the edge of a large field and

55

follows the course of Mor Brook. When Mor Brook bends away to the left keep forward over a stile and walk up a short gravel track to arrive at a bend in a crossing road. Turn left and pass under a bridge which carries the Severn Valley Railway over the road.

The line connects Hampton with Bridgnorth and is maintained by a dedicated group of railway enthusiasts. The short but pleasant journey through splendid countryside enables people to sample the almost forgotten age of steam.

Pass the entrance gates of Astbury Hall then gradually climb along the road. There are footpaths to right and left now. Turn left and follow a macadam lane towards Dinney Farm. Walk forward past a turn off to the right which goes to the farmhouse and continue to where the lane bends to the left towards a dwelling 200 metres away. Leave the lane to the right now, pass through a small gate, and climb along a hedged-in track. At the top of this short climb Chelmarsh Reservoir comes into view. Go through a facing gate and descend along a track.

Looking back across the reservoir, the tiny square tower of Chelmarsh church can be seen sitting proudly at the head of this vast expanse of man-made water.

Over to the right is a great banking which forms the reservoir dam. Go over stepping stones in a crossing stream then walk forward along a macadam lane. Cross a cattle grid and keep forward, ignoring turn-offs to the left. Emerge at a bend in a crossing lane in which keep left and walk past farms. Follow the lane as it turns and descends, pass under the Severn Valley Railway once again, then a little further on you are back at the parking area and the car.

STOKESAY

★

3 miles (5 km)

OS map 137

Craven Arms is well known as an agricultural marketing centre and autumn sheep sales attract large enthusiastic crowds. But for me the main attraction is the charming fortified manor house of Stokesay Castle, which lies close by the A49 to the south of the town. This medieval gem was built during the thirteenth century and boasts a fine timbered gatehouse, banqueting hall and Norman tower. There is also a church to add the finishing touch to a scene of historic splendour.

Leave the car at Stokesay Castle carpark, but before putting your boots on enjoy the medieval splendour to be seen inside the manor house. (Grid reference: 435 818).

On leaving the carpark, walk past the manor house, then go through a gate on the right almost opposite the stone tower. There is a large pond on your left as you follow a track which shortly takes you under the railway and into a large field. Turn right, and after 80 metres walk to the left of a field gate, then proceed, keeping a hedgerow on your immediate right. At the field corner go over a stile at the right of a facing field gate from which a derelict dwelling can be seen across the field over to the left. Still keeping the hedge on your right continue along the field edge and after 100 metres go over a short length of fencing on the right. Keeping a hedgerow on your right gradually descend in the direction of Craven Arms which can be seen straight ahead.

At the field corner join a track and carry on through a facing gate. This hedged-in track takes you under the railway. A rough lane goes past dwellings and leads to a crossing road. Go over it and turn right at the Stokesay Castle Hotel. A few yards along School Road brings you to Newton, a lane going off to the right. Pass the fine black and white Old Rectory and an interesting mixture of cottages. This tiny hamlet, which is the original settlement of Craven Arms, has retained much charm from a bygone age.

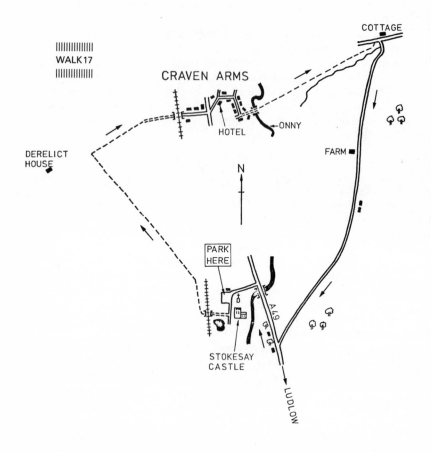

Turn left at the end of this short lane where a narrow way takes you between cottages and a modern dwelling, to a foot-bridge over the Onny. Cross the bridge and pause to take your bearings for the next part of the journey. With your back to the footbridge, look straight ahead across the facing field. There is a tiny red-brick house almost hidden by a large tree about 700 metres away; aim just to the right of this house and walk across the facing field to arrive at a crossing hedge. There is a small stream on the right and when I passed this way there was a tiny plank-bridge crossing it.

Go over a stile in the facing hedgerow/fence and walk forward, keeping the stream on your right about 25 metres away. Over to the left can be seen the red-brick house which you previously used as a marker. A cottage comes into view at the end of the field. Walk towards it and at the field corner go over a stout stile which takes you on to a crossing road where the way is right. Turn right again just before the cottage to enter a hedged-in lane.

Follow the lane past farm and dwelling until, after one mile, you emerge at a crossing road. Go over it and turn right to follow the roadside pavement. A short stroll takes you back to Stokesay and the car.

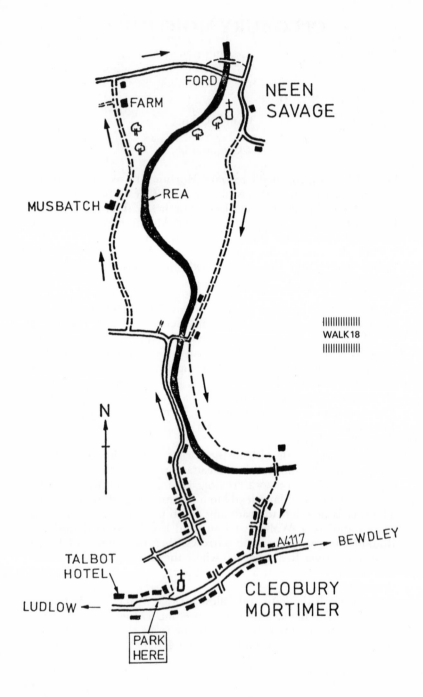

NEEN
SAVAGE

FORD

FARM

REA

MUSBATCH

WALK 18

N

TALBOT
HOTEL

A4117 → BEWDLEY

LUDLOW ←

CLEOBURY
MORTIMER

PARK
HERE

CLEOBURY MORTIMER

WALK 18

★

3 miles (5 km)

OS map 138

When I first approached Cleobury Mortimer I was reminded of a similar view in the Derbyshire town of Chesterfield, for both places have similar trademarks – churches with crooked spires. However, there is more to Cleobury Mortimer than initially meets the eye, as this short walk will reveal.

Park the car on the A4117 (Church Street), between the Talbot Hotel and the church with the crooked spire. (Grid reference: 673 757).

Walk up to the church. The way is now left along a path which follows the edge of the church confines via Castle Hill, but first of all take a peep inside the Church of St Mary the Virgin. The tower is 800 years old and on its top sits the famous crooked spire, the twisting probably resulting from warping of its oak frame and shingles. The east window is dedicated to the memory of William Langland, author of *The Vision Concerning Piers the Plowman*, who is said to have been born in the village in 1332. The church is full of interest and its history is recorded on a framed manuscript.

Proceed up Castle Hill to the corner of the church confines. Enter a narrow hedged-in macadam path on the left which quickly takes you on to a crossing lane where the way is right. Pass a school. The lane leads to a T-junction 150 metres away. The way is now left to gradually climb past cottages of varying shapes and sizes. Walk past Langland Road, Orchard End and Ronhill Crescent. The lane narrows, then descends and passes close to the river Rea. Bear left where the lane forks and climb for 200 metres to arrive at a gate on the right; a sign close by says 'Musbatch'.

Go through the gate and follow a track. After ¼ mile pass to the right of a black and white dwelling (Musbatch). Enter a hedged-in track now which goes to the right of outbuildings. Go through a gate and gradually climb for 400 metres to emerge by a farm. Go through a facing gate and walk forward along a track which takes you on to a crossing lane where there is a bungalow on the right. Turn right and after 400 metres arrive at a ford across the river. When I passed this way the river was in flood and I was thankful to use a footbridge which allowed me safe passage across.

Turn right beyond the river and climb past Neen Savage vicarage. The church is close by, but it may well be locked.

The lane turns to the left 60 metres beyond the church. Enter a hedged-in track on the right which takes you close by the river and goes past a building which sits close by the water. Shortly, there is a delightful dwelling on the left and a footbridge on the right. Keep straight ahead now and stay on the left side of the river where a facing gate gives access to a narrow riverside field. Keep on level terrain at the base of a banking on the left.

Follow the path as it turns to the left. After ¼ mile go over a footbridge on the right which takes you to the other side of the river, climb up a well worn path and go through a kissing gate. A short stretch of gravel path takes you on to a facing road close to dwellings. Walk straight ahead and, after 70 metres, turn left at a junction of roads beyond which a straight descent of 150 metres leads to a crossing road. Go over the road and turn right to follow the roadside pavement.

Pass the Bell Inn and walk back to the car which is parked close to the crooked spire.

BROMFIELD AND LUDLOW

WALK 19

★

6 miles (9.5 km)

OS map 137

Bromfield lies close by the A49 at its junction with the A4113, but only a small percentage of those rushing by ever stops to admire the village's fine medieval church and gaze from its tiny bridge over the Teme at scenes little changed over many long years. Bromfield also holds the key to a most interesting pedestrian approach to the beautiful and historic country town of Ludlow, so the combination of both places during the course of one walk should satisfy both walker and historian alike.

Park the car at the side of the road before an old gatehouse which, sadly, is all that remains of a former twelfth century Benedictine Priory. (Grid reference: 481 768).

The church is close by and, of its many interesting features, the most exuberant is its chancel roof which was painted over 200 years ago in a most flamboyant style. Walk past the gatehouse then linger on the tiny bridge over the Teme and admire a most charming view of the church. Pass to the right of a small lodge which gives access to Oakly Park. The bridleway, which has a macadam surface, takes you through a parkland setting. Over to the left is an imposing Georgian house which seems to be the ideal type of residence for such pleasant surroundings. Pass turn-offs to left and right and keep forward along an avenue of trees. Follow the bridleway as it dips and climbs.

Pass an isolated dwelling with a colonnaded porch, then continue through the tiny farming hamlet of Priors Halton. For the next mile your journey is via a lane which takes you through rich farming country and then affords a delightful view of Ludlow, with castle and church dominant. The lane emerges at a crossing road in which turn left past Clive Cottages to arrive at Dinham Bridge over the river Teme and which gives access to Ludlow town.

Ludlow has much to offer the enquiring visitor. The town was established towards the end of the eleventh century and grew

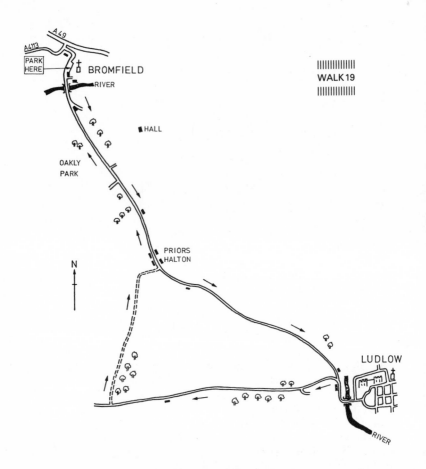

prosperous due, initially, to a flourishing wool trade. Ludlow Castle, which dominates the western approaches, was built towards the end of the twelfth century and from its towers there are many interesting views over the town and surrounding countryside. Close by a small museum is the parish church which was built on a grand scale and contains excellent medieval carvings. The Feathers Hotel, which has stood in Corve Street for almost 300 years, is one of the best half-timbered buildings in all England. Wander along High Street, Broad Street, Old Street, Camp Lane and St John's Lane and absorb the atmosphere of one of the finest country towns in Britain.

Return to Dinham Bridge and once again walk back past Clive Cottages. Keep forward past the lane from which you emerged earlier and follow the road as it climbs and turns to the left. After 350 metres the road turns very sharply to the left, but keep forward here and enter a tree-lined lane headed by a No Through Road sign. Follow this very pleasant and secluded lane for one mile to where, on the right and opposite a field gate, there is a public footpath sign and a stile.

Turn right here and leave the lane; there are ferns and trees on your right. Descend across a large field, then go through a gate set in a crossing hedge 60 metres from the field corner and follow a track along the next field edge. The track becomes hedged in on both sides and leads to a crossing lane via a stile. Turn left and once again pass through Priors Halton, then retrace your original route through Oakly Park and on back to Bromfield and the car.

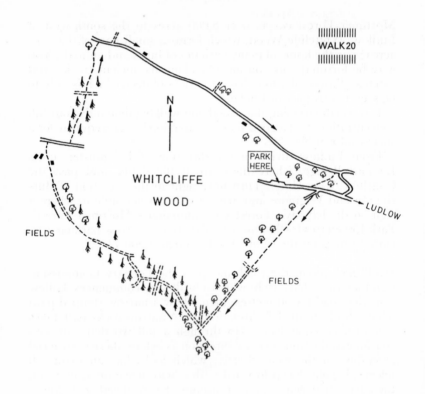

WALK 20

N

WHITCLIFFE
WOOD

PARK
HERE

LUDLOW

FIELDS

FIELDS

WHITCLIFFE WOOD

WALK 20

★

3½ miles (5.5 km)

OS map 138

Mortimer Forest covers over 8,000 acres to the south-west of Ludlow. Whitcliffe Wood, which forms a small part of this vast acreage, is the home of many varieties of birds and animals. You may be fortunate, as you journey along its ancient tracks, and catch a glimpse of a long haired variety of deer which is only to be seen is this part of England.

It is worth stressing that woodland walking demands your full concentration, and a good sense of direction is a prerequisite for a successful ramble.

From Ludlow, drive in the direction of Leominster, cross Ludford Bridge, where there are traffic lights, and pass the Charlton Arms Hotel. Turn next right in the direction of Burrington and Wigmore and drive for almost one mile to where a sign on the left says 'Forestry Commission – Mortimer Forest'. Park 150 metres further on, where there is a narrow parking area close to trees on the right. (Grid reference: 500 744).

Walk back along the road and pass the Forestry Commission sign then turn sharp right where a bridleway commences. Follow a service road for 30 metres, then follow a narrow stepped path which climbs to the left through trees. A narrow rocky path takes you to a crossing fence. Go through a tall wooden gate and continue in the same general direction as before; there is an aerial assembly on the right shortly, which looks like an extra tall telegraph pole. Keep forward with a wire fence on your right, then pass between a pair of stumps. Keep ahead to follow a sunken track.

Many of these tracks were made by charcoal burners' carts as the ancient art of charcoal burning only ceased in this area about 50 years ago.

Navigational concentration is required shortly. There is a fence on the left which turns sharply to the left but a few yards before this there is a junction of tracks on your right. Turn right, almost at a right-angle. There is a track going off diagonally to the right, but ignore this and walk forward along a sunken path at the commencement of which are evergreens on the right and deciduous trees on the left, but after 50 metres the trees on both sides are evergreens. This well-worn path shortly meets a major crossing track. Go straight across it and continue along a sunken way and, after 120 metres, turn right at a T-junction of tracks. Arrive on another track via steps. Turn left and continue. The trees on the left give way to fields and the track becomes a path and then emerges on to a well-worn track. Walk forward along it and pass an exposed bank of rock on the left until a facing gate gives access to a field.

There are now delightful vistas across Mary Knoll Valley and ahead to Bringewood Chase.

Keep forward, gradually descend along the field edge, and pass close to an outbuilding via a pair of stiles. There is a dwelling on the left now, surrounded by a hedgerow. A facing field gate gives access to a crossing road where the way is right but after 70 metres leave the road on the left where a path takes you on an ever-increasing descent through trees. Go straight over a crossing track. A tiny gate gives access to a large undulating field. Descend in the same direction as before and follow a line of telegraph poles.

The humpback form of Wenlock Edge can be seen straight ahead across the Teme Valley.

A gate takes you on to a crossing lane where the way is right. Follow this pleasantly secluded lane for over a mile to where, on the right, there is a footpath which climbs diagonally to the right. This footpath commences 60 metres before a bend in a crossing road is reached. Climb through trees and undergrowth to emerge onto a crossing road. Turn right and walk back to the car which is parked 120 metres away.

VALE OF LLANGOLLEN

★

7¼ miles (11.5 km)

OS map 117

'The Pontcysyllte Aqueduct is the most impressive work of art that I have ever laid my eyes upon.' This was Sir Walter Scott's reaction to Thomas Telford's masterpiece of civil engineering which carries the Llangollen branch of the Shropshire Union Canal high above the river Dee in the beautiful Vale of Llangollen. During the course of this walk you will be able to inspect Telford's work at close quarters, as a 'concessionary' path allows us to cross the aqueduct.

Leave the car at Froncysyllte, on a parking area adjacent to the canal just down the hill from the Aqueduct Inn, and off the road which connects the A5 with the A539. (Grid reference: 270 415).

On leaving the car, turn right and follow the canal towpath to a footbridge at the side of a counter-balanced roadbridge. Cross the canal here, and turn left to continue along the towpath opposite to where the car is parked. The canal is tree-lined here and is raised above the surrounding countryside on a high embankment. As you emerge from the trees, commence the traverse of the aqueduct. There is a guard rail for walkers along the towpath, but people in boats have a more precarious crossing as there is no protection at all on the other side.

The aqueduct is over 1,000 ft long and carries the canal 127 ft above the river. Telford's design was unique as it consisted of a cast-iron trough supported on a row of tall stone piers. Construction commenced in 1795 and the first boat crossed it in 1805. The total cost was £47,000.

On completing the crossing turn right and leave the towpath to follow a path which goes underneath the aqueduct. This is a good vantage point from which to inspect the cast-iron trough in detail. The path leads to a road. Turn left and descend, then turn right to follow a path which commences at the side of semi-detached dwellings. Climb up the path to arrive once again at a

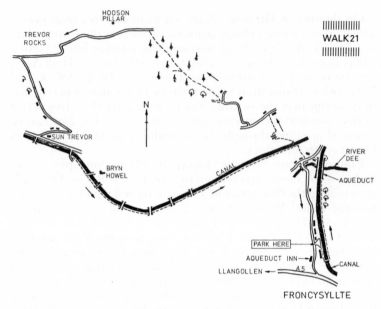

HOOSON
PILLAR

TREVOR
ROCKS

N

SUN TREVOR

BRYN
HOWEL

CANAL

RIVER
DEE

AQUEDUCT

PARK HERE

AQUEDUCT INN

LLANGOLLEN ◄ — A5

CANAL

FRONCYSYLLTE

canal towpath and then cross the canal by a substantial foot-bridge.

The path leads diagonally left across a facing field. Cross a stile and then go through an underpass which takes you beneath a disused railway line. The path leads to a crossing road where the way is left. Follow the roadside footpath for 250 metres then turn next right along a winding lane which climbs away from the road. The lane turns to the left and then sharply to the right but leave the lane here and enter a tree-lined track through a facing gateway close by Gardener's Lodge. Care is now required in order not to miss the route.

Fifty metres after passing through the gateway turn right to follow a narrow path which climbs away from the track through trees. A sign here indicates Offa's Dyke Path. Follow the path as it climbs through the trees then skirt the edge of a long narrow field via a pair of stiles and continue through very dense forest. Even at the height of the summer this pathway is plunged into semi-darkness here because the trees are very densely planted. Fork right at a junction of paths and continue to climb and eventually emerge from the trees for a short distance at a point where there are magnificent views over the Vale of Llangollen. The path eventually leads on to a crossing lane via a stile. Turn left and walk along this exposed, elevated highway.

On the right is Hooson's Pillar – a memorial to a local poet – which affords a fine vantage point for views over the surrounding countryside. Straight ahead, surmounting a facing hill, is Castell Dinas Bran, a site on which a hill fort stood since the Dark Ages, but the present ruin dates from about 1200. To the left of, and 750 ft below Dinas Bran is the town of Llangollen, where a fine stone bridge over the swirling waters of the river Dee gives access to the town and the opposite side of the valley. The Dee can be observed winding through the beautiful Vale of Llangollen to Pontcysyllte Aqueduct.

Continue along the lane, known locally as 'precipice walk', and pass the large exposed outcrops of Trevor Rocks. One mile after joining the lane arrive at a lane on the left which leads down into the valley. Walk down this lane for a mile to arrive at the Sun Trevor Hotel where a crossing road is met. Across the road is the Llangollen Canal. Unfortunately, we cannot use the towpath here as this section is not a public path, so turn left and follow the roadside footpath parallel with the canal. After about ½ mile go over the next bridge on the right and continue along the towpath (now a public path). The canal passes close to the Bryn Howel Hotel then shortly, where the canal is raised above the level of the surrounding countryside, the towpath affords a really fine view across the river Dee on the right.

The towpath eventually leads back to the substantial footbridge which was crossed earlier in the walk. Turn right and descend along the path to the road.

There is an alternative now: *either* retrace your original route back to the car via the aqueduct; *or* turn right and follow the road around to the left where it crosses the river via a narrow stone bridge. This road leads back to Froncysyllte and the car.

71

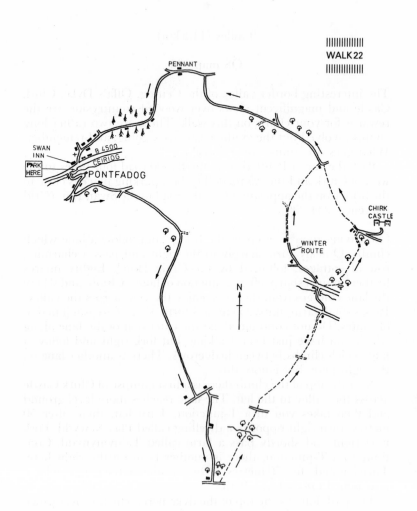

PENNANT

SWAN
INN

PARK
HERE

B 4500

CEIRIOG

PONTFADOG

CHIRK
CASTLE

WINTER
ROUTE

N

THE CEIRIOG VALLEY

WALK 22

★

9 miles (14.5 km)

OS map 126

The interesting border valley of the Ceiriog, Offa's Dyke, Chirk Castle and magnificent views over wooded countryside are the rewards for your efforts on this walk. There are two rather long climbs involved but the gradients are easy going, and remember: What goes up – must come down!

Park the car at Pontfadog by the B4500 road four miles to the west of Chirk and the A5 road. The best parking place is close to the bridge on the opposite side of the road to the Swan Inn. (Grid reference: 234 380).

On leaving the car, go over the bridge and follow a lane which climbs. Quickly turn sharply to the right and pass a charming row of cottages, followed by the Craig Hotel. Eighty metres further on turn sharp left at a junction of lanes. Climb, and where the lane emerges from the trees, enjoy the view across the valley. Pass a small farm, until 250 metres further on, there is a junction of routes. Do not continue along the extension of the lane along which you have just been walking, but fork right and follow a lane which climbs between hedgerows. There is another lane on the right here, but ignore this.

Near the top of the climb there is a first glimpse of Chirk Castle across the valley to the left. The lane reaches more level ground and then takes you to a T-junction. Turn left, then, after 50 metres, turn right opposite a dwelling called Plas Newydd. Fork next right and shortly pass a farm called Tainymynydd. Continue to a T-junction; there is another farm on the right here. Turn left and after 70 metres, go over a stile on the left. You have now joined Offa's Dyke Path.

The path follows the top of the dyke here, which is overgrown with bracken and gorse. There are magnificent long sweeping views shortly, across to Chirk Castle, and the aqueduct which carries the Llangollen branch of the Shropshire Union Canal across the valley floor. The next section of path is well-defined

73

and easy to follow but care is required through the Nant Eris ravine where there are steep gradients. The path leads to a crossing lane where the way is right and quickly left to continue along the line of the dyke. The path descends and leads straight over a crossing track. Keep to the left of a rough, sloping field now, and descend.

The view across to Chirk Castle could be one taken straight out of the pages of a history book.

Cross a number of stiles, then, halfway down the hill, enter a hedged-in track. Descend, then turn left prior to a facing dwelling and follow a path to a crossing road. Go over the road and descend along a lane which takes you over the river Ceiriog. Arrive at a crossing road close to St Catherine's Church.

There are two options now. *Either* follow an interesting route through the grounds of Chirk Castle prior to rejoining the official route (this permissive path is only open between April and September); *or* the official route which must be followed during the months between October and March. During summertime you therefore have a choice – but the route through the grounds of Chirk Castle is by far the more interesting and allows you to visit the castle if you so desire.

Route 1 (April to September only)
Enter the castle grounds through a gate under a small stone arch and follow a well worn path through trees. The path climbs and winds to a crossing fence. Cross this fence and climb forward keeping a fence and trees on your immediate left. Go through a gate and continue through trees and ferns to a track which joins the route from the right. Climb along this track to arrive at the entrance drive of the castle.

A visit to the castle will prove most rewarding. Completed during the reign of Edward II, it was, and still is, an extremely strong fortification. A detailed history can be obtained,inside.

Follow the entrance drive in the direction of the carpark and pass The House on the Dyke. Turn left prior to the carpark where a sign indicates 'Tyn-y-groes'. There is an old style farm on the left now. Go through a large gate and follow a track which skirts the edge of a large field. Pass through two further gates to join a lane where the way is forward. The official path joins this lane from the left. Continue from [*] on page 75.

Route 2 (Winter route)
From St Catherine's Church cross the road to enter a narrow lane which climbs diagonally away from the road. Continue to

where the lane forks and keep right. Climb, pass through out-buildings, and continue along a rough track. After 200 metres go over a stile on the right to enter a sloping field. Climb to the right of a stone wall then go over a stile at the left side of a field gate. Follow a track across the facing field and go over a couple of stiles to emerge onto the lane at Tyn-y-groes. Turn left and climb up the lane.

[*] Climb to where the lane forks by a dwelling called Wern Tower. Bear left in the direction of Pontfadog. Pass a rough track on the left, headed by a sign which says 'Unsuitable for motors'. Follow the lane as it dips and climbs for the next mile to arrive at a T-junction. Turn left and follow the lane through a farm called Pennant. Shortly, the lane forks; bear left here to wind and descend with splendid views across the Ceiriog Valley to the wooded hills beyond. Again, keep left where the lane forks and descend. The lane passes through quite dense forest and emerges on the outskirts of Pontfadog. The facing lane leads onto a crossing road close to the Swan Inn and the car.

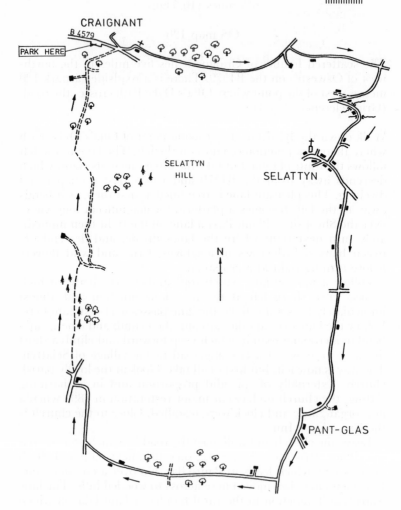

CRAIGNANT

B 4579

PARK HERE

SELATTYN
HILL

SELATTYN

N

PANT-GLAS

SELATTYN HILL AND PANT-GLAS

WALK 23

★

6½ miles (10.5 km)

OS map 126

The scattered hamlet of Craignant lies five miles to the north-west of Oswestry on the B4579. There is a roadside carpark 120 metres west of the point where Offa's Dyke Path crosses the road. (Grid reference: 253 349).

Walk down the B4579 to the crossing point of Offa's Dyke Path where there is a junction of lanes on the left. The lane to the left follows the route of Offa, but take the other one to its right, which descends away from the B4579 and winds past a chapel and dwelling. This pleasant lane is tree-lined at first then, as it bends away to the left, becomes a platform for magnificent long views over the Shropshire Plain. Pass a lane on the right then immediately turn next right where the lanes divide, and descend between banked hedgerows of foxgloves, ferns and wild flowers before turning right at a crossroads.

Follow a narrow lane which dips and weaves between high banks. Turn sharp left at the next lane junction and almost immediately pass a dwelling; the lane passes over a stream here. Follow the lane over another stream, then climb and emerge at a bend in a crossing road in which keep forward and climb a short distance to arrive at a crossing road in the village of Selattyn. The way is now left, but first of all take a look at the lovely parish church. Externally of splendid proportion and in a charming setting, the church underwent major restoration in 1892 when a new organ, aisle and clock were installed. Close to the church is the Cross-Keys Inn.

Leave the church and walk past the road by which you entered the village. Pass the schoolhouse, then turn next right and climb along a lane which leads to Pant-Glas. Go over a crossing lane. Fine views may be enjoyed here across to wooded hills. The lane leads to a T-junction in the rural hamlet of Pant-Glas in which turn left, then almost immediately fork right and climb in the direction of the 'Old Racecourse'. Turn next right and continue to climb. On passing a farm the lane becomes a rough track between hedgerows before leading to more level ground. Keep forward now along a metalled lane which eventually leads to a T-junction where the way is right.

If the day is clear, there are long views westwards now, towards the Berwyn Mountains.

The road descends to a T-junction close to a farm. Turn right in the direction of Selattyn, walk past a road which leads to Llechydau, then leave the road and go over a half-hidden stile up a bank on the left. You have now joined Offa's Dyke Path.

The ditch and bank of the Dyke can be clearly seen leading up the facing hillside; the footpath hugs the side of the Dyke and there are various stiles to negotiate. Follow the path as it skirts the edge of a large wood and, on leaving it, follow a field edge, then go over a crossing stream via a footbridge. The path leads to a farm entrance drive. Turn right here, go over a cattle grid, then turn sharp left and go over a stile to follow a track which climbs up the facing hillside. Over to the right is the wooded crest of Selattyn Hill.

There are magnificent views in all directions here, over rolling wooded countryside.

Near the top of the climb, enter a field over a stile on your left. Bear right across the field, then descend, to turn right at a fence corner. Go over a stile and continue along a grassy track where there are crumbling stone walls on both sides. Join a facing half-macadamed lane close by a farm called Woodside. Cross a stile.

A short descent leads to the B4579 road at Craignant. Turn left and walk back to the car which is parked close by.

RACE COURSE HILL

WALK 24

★

7¼ miles (11.5 km)

OS map 126

In years gone by, the townspeople of Oswestry spent many a happy summer afternoon at the racecourse of Llawnt, set on a hilltop a couple of miles to the west of the town. Today, the old racecourse is a common, where attractive parking facilities have been laid out amidst the gorse and heather. This carpark is 550 metres south of the B4580 in the direction of Treflach and Trefonen. (Grid reference: 257 307).

Follow a path which commences at the southern end of the carpark. Quickly join the wide grassy expanse of the old race-course. Keep forward where the racecourse turns to the right and join Offa's Dyke Path at a stile by a row of tall conifers. Pass through a wood, go over a stile, then descend through ferns and trees to a crossing track. Go through a gate on the right. The tracks fork; the right-hand one descends, but follow the left-hand track which stays on more level terrain. Emerge from the trees and walk along a high terrace where the hillside drops away sharply on the right. On the left is the Dyke itself, which is in a fine state of preservation, whilst to the right the hillside drops sharply away to the floor of the valley. This area abounds with wildlife, there being many varied species of flowers and trees.

The path leads past the concave stone slab known as 'Offa's Seat', then meanders through trees. A rather pleasant resting place will be found on the left now, where a stone seat is protected by an overhanging roof. The path descends through trees. Turn right at a crossing path, then left to follow a rocky path. Go over a crossing fence and emerge from the trees. Follow a facing track past a dwelling and arrive at a crossing lane via a gate.

Cross the lane, go over a footbridge, then join a lane close by The Old Mill Inn. Climb along the lane, walk over a crossing road, and enter a field via a stile. Follow the field edge in the direction of the Dyke which can be seen straight ahead. The path

79

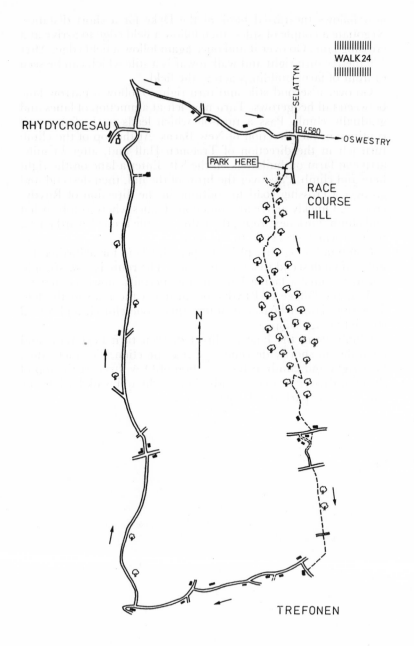

WALK 24

RHYDYCROESAU

SELATTYN

B4580 → OSWESTRY

PARK HERE

RACE
COURSE
HILL

N

TREFONEN

now follows the raised bank of the Dyke for a short distance. Negotiate a couple of stiles, then follow a field edge to arrive at a crossing lane. Go over it and once again follow a field edge. After 100 metres turn right and walk towards a stile which can be seen in front of farm buildings across the field.

Go over a second stile and turn right to follow a narrow lane between tall hedgerows. Turn next left at a junction of lanes and gradually climb. Pass a turn-off which leads to Trefonen and continue in the direction of New Barns. At the top of the climb turn left in the direction of Trefonen Hall and, after ¼ mile, arrive at farm outbuildings on the left. Enter a lane on the right here and climb. Pass over the brow of the hill, then descend and go over a crossing road to continue in the direction of Rhydy-croesau. Quickly arrive at a junction of lanes where you bear left and climb. Fork next right, then after ¼ mile keep forward past a turn-off which descends to the right.

Continue along this pleasant peaceful lane for a further 1¼ miles, then descend to a crossing road. The route is now straight ahead to enter a facing lane. If time permits, however, have a look at the village of Rhydycroesau down the road to the left. This tiny hamlet boasts an interesting stone church and a well stocked village shop.

Climb along the lane as directed, then turn next right and continue, to shortly descend to a road junction. Turn left, then bear right and climb in the direction of Oswestry. At the top of the climb arrive at a crossroads. Turn right and walk back to the car, which is parked 550 metres away.

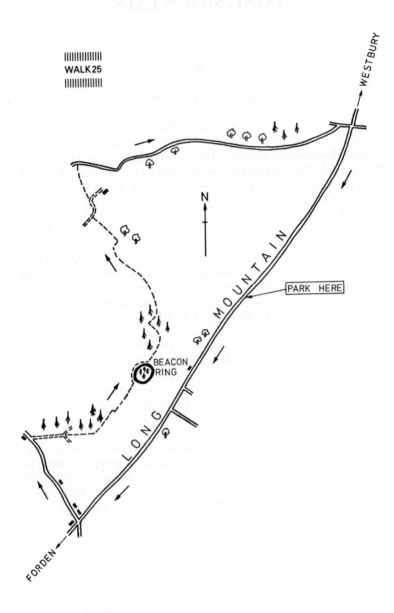

WESTBURY

N

LONG MOUNTAIN

PARK HERE

BEACON
RING

FORDEN

LONG MOUNTAIN

WALK 25

★

6½ miles (10.5 km)

OS map 126

Long Mountain dominates the Severn Valley to the east of Welshpool. The intriguing ancient hill-fort of Beacon Ring sits atop the summit and presents a fine vantage point for commanding views over the surrounding hills, valleys and the Shropshire Plain. It is an exposed place in winter, but each season brings a different-looking landscape and it is an interesting area to explore.

A lane climbs and runs along the backbone of Long Mountain, connecting Forden with Westbury. The highest point of this lane is some 3½ miles from Forden and six miles from Westbury. Leave the car at the side of the road here, where there is good verge parking. (Grid reference: 274 067).

Walk along the lane in a south-westerly direction, that is to say, in the direction of Forden. Keep forward past a lane which goes off to the left, to where, after almost a further mile, there is a junction of lanes. The lane on the left leads to Marton whilst that straight ahead goes to Forden; but turn right in the direction of Welshpool. Descend, and after ½ mile pass a stile on the left where Offa's Dyke Path meets the lane.

The lane climbs slightly to a brow which affords long views towards Welshpool. Turn sharp right here, just before a farm on the left is reached, and climb along a narrow lane which leads into a track that forks to either side of a facing gate. Go through this gate and climb along a field edge and go over a stile at the field corner.

Pause here and look back to admire some magnificent views over the Severn Valley.

There is now a gentle climb ahead, of 600 metres up to the summit of Long Mountain and the hill-fort of Beacon Ring. This circular earthwork, of massive construction, surrounds a plantation of beech and pine trees planted in 1953. This is the highest point on today's walk, at 1,339 ft above sea level.

The path continues through a conifer wood and turns left, and then right. Emerge from the trees at a stile which leads into a large rough field in which bear diagonally left and walk to a stile at the end of the field. Go over and descend along a rough grassy track.

Over to the right, if the day is clear, there are extremely long views along the Severn Valley towards Oswestry and beyond. In the near distance the Breidden Hills can be seen, with the monument on top of Rodney's Pillar dominant.

A stile leads on to the open hillside. Descend and go over another stile then proceed, keeping a fence on your immediate right. Go over a crossing fence and follow the path to a crossing track. Turn right through a gateway and follow the track as it turns to left and right. Leave the track on the left here, where a stile gives access to a field. Follow the path along a field edge and arrive at a crossing lane in which turn right and climb along the lane.

Climb for over a mile to where, shortly after passing a joining lane from the left, there is a junction of lanes. A sign at the head of the facing lane says 'Weight Limit 2 Tons – One Mile Ahead', but turn right here and gradually climb to more level terrain between banked hedgerows. A gentle stroll now, of ¾ mile, leads back to the car.

LEIGHTON PARK

WALK 26

★

5½ miles (9 km)

OS map 126

Today's jaunt will take you through the glorious wooded scenery of Leighton Park, an extremely interesting estate located on the side of Long Mountain and overlooking the beautiful Severn Valley.

Four miles to the south of Welshpool is the scattered village of Forden, the bulk of which straddles the A490 and B4388 roads. The A490 leaves the B4388 where a roadsign indicates Church Stoke and Chirbury. Park the car 250 metres from this junction where there are roadside parking facilities on the left-hand side of the road. (Grid reference: 240 019).

Walk back towards the B4388 then, 70 metres before the road junction, go over a fence by a farm on the right; you have now joined Offa's Dyke Path.

The route is along the line of the Dyke, which can be seen as a raised mound and follows field edges and over stiles to a crossing lane. Turn left, then right, and take a rough gravel track which quickly turns away to the right. Keep straight ahead, however, where a narrow hedged-in path leads to a field. Follow the field edge then go over two stiles to enter a lane. Turn right and follow the lane as it climbs. After ½ mile leave the lane and enter a track on the left where a nameboard indicates Greenwood Lodge. Follow the right-hand track past a small lodge house. The path gradually climbs through trees and leads on to a joining track from the right. Keep forward and proceed along level terrain. Over to the left shortly, and through the trees, are long views over Leighton Park and Leighton Hall can be seen, with a church dominant.

The Hall and park were originally owned by John Naylor, a Victorian banker from Liverpool, who bought the estate in 1849. Naylor had a great affection for 'monkey puzzle trees' and these can be observed all over the estate. He also pursued many agricultural and engineering innovations and remnants of his

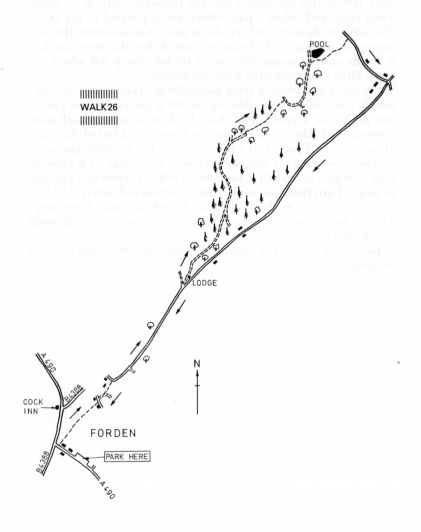

WALK 26

hydro-power schemes can be seen in the form of man-made pools.

Keep right where the track forks and gradually climb. The bank of Offa's Dyke is in evidence on the immediate left here and after 100 metres the path turns left through a gap in its bank. Turn right and follow a path which keeps parallel to the Dyke. The path leads over level terrain at first, then descends through trees to a crossing track. Turn right and follow this forest track as it bends around to the left over a bridge. Keep left where the track forks, and pass over a second bridge.

On the left shortly, a truly magnificent specimen of 'monkey puzzle tree' will be seen. Also on the left is the overgrown ruin of one of Naylor's pools. The track leads to a second and more obvious pool. Do not follow the track past the head of this pool. Instead, keep forward to follow a rough track which gradually climbs through trees and undergrowth to emerge at a crossing lane in which turn right. Climb for ½ mile to arrive at a junction of lanes. Turn right and walk in the direction of Forden. The lane gently climbs then descends past Woodside, and Greenwood Lodge, which is where you commenced your walk through Leighton Park.

Keep forward and descend along the lane, then retrace your original route back to the car.

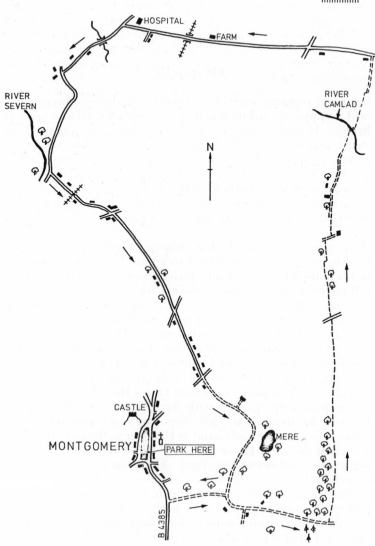

HOSPITAL

FARM

RIVER
SEVERN

RIVER
CAMLAD

N

CASTLE

MERE

MONTGOMERY

PARK HERE

B 4385

MONTGOMERY

WALK 27

★

8½ miles (13.5 km)

OS map 137·

Before the reorganisation of our county boundaries, Montgomery held a unique record in that it was the smallest county town in Britain. However, boundary changes have not removed its charm and a visit to this border gem should not be missed. A rocky crag on the edge of town was the site of a medieval castle – alas now in ruins – but a visit to the ruins and a stroll around the town are a pleasant prelude to the walk.

Park the car on the wide expanse of road aptly named Broad Street, in front of the town hall. (Grid reference: 223 964).

On leaving the car, walk along Bishop's Castle Street, pass the Crown Inn and continue past Tan-y-mur. Follow the road as it bends to the left, pass a road which goes off to the left, and, after 120 metres follow a track on the left which is headed by a sign indicating Offa's Dyke. Go through a couple of gates to arrive at a crossing metalled lane. Turn right and shortly pass Montgomery Cricket Club. The lane takes you over a cattle grid and on through a pleasant parkland setting. The lane passes through a wood after which the raised bank of Offa's Dyke can be seen in the fields on the right. Go over a cattle grid and turn left to follow a field edge. You have now joined Offa's Dyke Path.

The path keeps parallel with the Dyke which is in evidence between the trees on the left. Negotiate stiles and follow field edges with a fine view of Corndon Hill over to the right from this section of the path. Leave the trees behind and continue with a hedge on your immediate right. Montgomery, together with church and castle, comes into view across the fields.

The footpath follows the Dyke ditch, then passes close to a well preserved section of bank and leads to a crossing road. Go straight across it and continue along field edges via gates. Turn right at a field corner where a stile leads through a gap in the bank of the Dyke, then turn left and continue along the Dyke. At the field corner go over a stile, turn right and follow a track which

89

takes you towards a small farm. Just before the farm is reached a stile on the left gives access to a field. Continue, keeping a fence on the right and go through a facing gate to walk past ruinous cottages. One can well imagine the isolated existence led by the former occupants of these cottages.

The route continues along a wide, grassy hedged-in track, a gate at the end of which leads into a large field. Keep forward with a hedge on your immediate right. Pass over the river Camlad via a substantial footbridge. Turn left and continue, again keeping a hedge on your immediate right. After 200 metres go over a plank-bridge and stile and continue along a track. Arrive at a crossing lane via gates. Turn left and climb along the lane. You have now left Offa's Dyke Path. Go straight over a crossing road. Pass Woodlands Farm, cross the railway and arrive at a T-junction close by a country hospital. Turn left here and descend, then once again cross over the Camlad via a bridge. There is a small but quite charming cottage on the left now.

Follow the lane as it bends to the left opposite the entrance to a large detached dwelling where there is a minor turn off to the right, but keep left as directed. Descend, then follow the lane as it turns sharply to the right and keep forward for ½ mile to where the lane runs close by the river Severn, which can be seen through trees on the right. This was the site of a Roman occupation, although unfortunately there are no visible remains of their presence.

Turn next left and walk up to a level crossing which can be seen straight ahead. Cross the railway, taking great care to observe the written instructions, then gradually climb past dwellings to arrive at a junction of lanes. Go straight over the crossing lane and descend.

Follow a delightful, winding lane for ¾ mile. Go straight over a crossing road and continue past large detached dwellings, cross a road and enter a narrow lane where a sign indicates a footpath. After ¼ mile pass a farm entrance drive, then keep forward over a cattle grid. The lane turns to the right, then bends to the left. A large mere can be seen down on the left here, and the area abounds with wildlife. Pass over a cattle grid before leaving the lane 50 metres farther on where there is a gate on the right.

You have now joined part of your original route. Follow the facing track which takes you back to Montgomery and the car.

EDENHOPE HILL

WALK 28

★

7½ miles (12 km)

OS map 137

On a warm summer's day the hills to the west of Bishop's Castle provide excellent walking. Spring and autumn also bring their delights, but during winter these same hills take on a different mood when the famous Clun Forest sheep, which are to be seen roaming the area in abundance, are thankful for their warm woolly overcoats. Although somewhat remote, the area is criss-crossed by numerous minor lanes so careful navigation is re-quired in order to arrive at the parking place.

From Bishop's Castle drive along a minor road which leaves the B4385 between the church and the Six Bells Inn – where a sign points in the direction of Bishop's Moat (2) and Mainstone (4). After 1¾ miles turn left at a T-junction. A straight ½ mile leads past a fine example of a motte and bailey mound on the right. A little further on is a junction of lanes. Drive in the direction of Pantglas and Hopton. Almost 1½ miles further on are staggered crossroads followed by a telephone box. Drive forward for almost ¾ mile to where Offa's Dyke Path crosses the lane via a pair of stiles. Park the car 80 metres further on, where there is good verge parking available on the left. (Grid reference: 257 896).

On leaving the car, walk back to Offa's Dyke Path and go over the stile on your right. Quickly cross a second stile, then follow the path along the top of the Dyke bank. Negotiate two further stiles, before descending through a wood. Emerge from it at a stile which leads onto a crossing track. Turn left, then after 80 metres turn right and traverse the stream-like river Unk via a tiny plank bridge. Turn left and after 120 metres bear right and begin to climb along the Dyke bank where there is a fence on the right. Go over a fence-stile and continue to climb. Rest for a while at the top of the climb and admire a lovely view across the partly wooded valley you have just traversed.

A stile takes you on to a narrow metalled lane. Leave Offa's

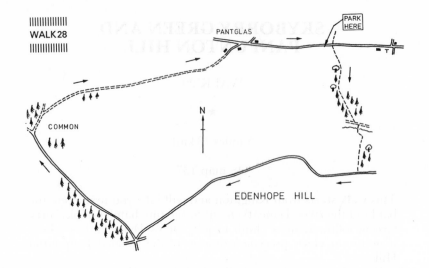

Dyke Path now and turn right to walk along the lane and follow
it for two miles and admire fine panoramic views on the way.
Arrive at a junction of lanes where you turn sharp right and walk
at the side of a large conifer plantation called Ceri. After 1¼
miles a large common on the right is a purple sea when the
heather is in bloom. Turn right shortly and continue with the
heather common on your right. The lane becomes a rough track
skirting the edge of the heather common. Keep forward past a
gated track which goes off to the left. Pass through a facing gate
and continue with a fence on the left and row of hawthorn trees
on the right. The track is quite rough here, but on passing
through a second gate the track is well defined and fenced in.

There is a fine view now across to the mass of Corndon Hill,
rising six miles away to a height approaching 1,700 ft.

Keep forward and follow the well defined track for one mile to
where it becomes a metalled lane. Descend to a junction of lanes
at the tiny farming hamlet of Pantglas. Turn right and gradually
climb, then, after 100 metres, fork right and pass a bungalow.
There are long views down the valley on the right now.

A further ½ mile along this pleasant lane takes you back to the
car.

SKYBORRY GREEN AND PANPUNTON HILL

WALK 29

★

5 miles (8 km)

OS map 137

This walk starts from Knighton and will take you first along the banks of the river Teme, then out to the tiny hamlet of Skyborry Green, followed by a climb to join Offa's Dyke Path – where magnificent views precede a descent of the wooded Panpunton Hill.

Drive down Crabtree Walk which leaves West Street at the side of the Youth Hostel and leave the car on Offa's Dyke Heritage Centre carpark. (Grid reference: 285 726).

On leaving the car, pass through a small gate at the corner of the carpark and follow a level path, parallel with the river which is half-hidden by trees on the right. Keep forward past steps on the left, then pass through three kissing gates in quick succession. Follow a pleasant riverside footpath, then go over a wooden footbridge across the river. Go over the railway line (take great care here) and follow a path to a crossing lane. Turn left and walk along the lane. Shortly, you will pass the entrance drive of Weir Cottage, which was where Lord Hunt lived when he was chosen as leader of the first successful Everest expedition.

After a further mile, arrive at a junction of lanes. To the left is Lloyney and Llanvair Waterdine, but turn right in the direction of Clun and Selley Cross and almost immediately turn right again to follow a track between a farmhouse and outbuildings. Pass Herb Cottage, then go through a gateway and climb to the left of a dwelling and outbuildings. Follow the track as it climbs between banks. Turn left at a dwelling called The Brynny, pass through a gate, turn sharply to right and left, then continue along the track which climbs close by hawthorn trees and leads over the open hillside. Twenty metres before a facing gateway is reached, go over a stile on the right. You have now joined Offa's Dyke Path.

The ditch and bank of Offa's Dyke are very much in evidence

93

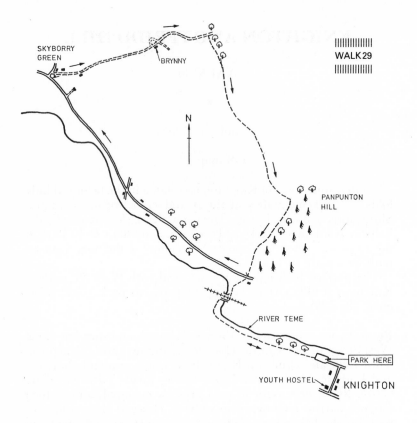

here, whilst the elevated position of this section of the path affords magnificent views over the surrounding countryside. In the valley down on the right is the village of Knucklas while the high mound to the right of the railway viaduct is the site where Knucklas Castle once stood.

The route continues over generally level terrain and takes you over a number of stiles. After a mile or so there are fine views over Knighton and the winding river Teme. The path gradually descends towards the woods on the side of Panpunton Hill. Turn sharp right before the trees are reached and descend along a steep grassy track to a crossing lane. Go over this lane and cross a stile, then follow the riverside path which you negotiated earlier in the walk to arrive back at the carpark and the car.

KNIGHTON AND FFRIDD HILL

WALK 30

★

4¾ miles (7.5 km)

OS map 137

The interesting town of Knighton is situated in the beautiful hilly folds of the Teme Valley at the boundary between Powys and Shropshire. Known as the 'Town on the Dyke', it marks the halfway point on Offa's Dyke Footpath, and Offa's Dyke Park in the town was where the opening ceremony of the long-distance path took place in 1971.

The parking instructions are identical with Walk 29; park in Knighton at Offa's Dyke Heritage Centre car park. (Grid reference: 285 726).

Retrace your route back to the youth hostel, and turn left along West Street to arrive at the clock tower in the centre of the town. Turn right and climb up High Street which gradually narrows and leads to Market Street and Castle Road. Turn left along Castle Road, bear right to pass brightly coloured houses, then follow a narrow lane between cottages. Descend along a narrow path on the left, where there is a barrier down the centre, to arrive at a crossing lane. Turn right and follow the lane past many interesting old cottages, some of which are set on lower ground on the left.

Emerge at a T-junction where the way is left. Turn right at the road ahead, pass a garage, then turn left and follow a narrow lane which gradually climbs away from the road past farm and dwelling, to where, shortly after passing The Tiled House, there is a T-junction. Turn left, pass a farm, then go over a stile on the left in a hedgerow 50 metres before a junction of lanes is reached. You have now joined Offa's Dyke Path.

The path faithfully follows the Dyke here, and is very thoroughly way-marked. The route takes you over field and stile up the gentle ascent of Ffridd Hill. The Dyke is on a massive scale, as you will see on your immediate right as you ascend the hill, and gives an idea of the size of the original construction.

From the top of Ffridd Hill long views can be enjoyed in all

95

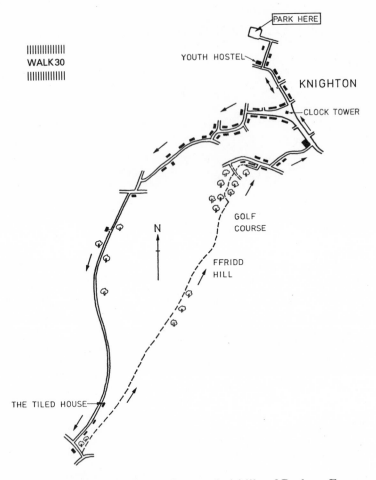

|||||||||||||
WALK 30
|||||||||||||

PARK HERE

YOUTH HOSTEL

KNIGHTON

CLOCK TOWER

GOLF COURSE

N

FFRIDD HILL

THE TILED HOUSE

directions; at the far left are the wooded hills of Radnor Forest, whilst to the right, if the day is clear, Clee Hill can be seen. The hill, which is over twenty miles away, dominates the landscape to the east of Ludlow and was the site of an Iron Age hill-fort where now the white duo of radio beacons rear up.

The path descends and skirts the edge of Knighton golf course. On the left is Great Ffrydd Wood, to which a stile shortly gives access. Descend through trees then go over a crossing lane. The path emerges at the rear of houses. Walk forward, then turn left between the houses and arrive opposite Ffrydd Terrace. Turn right and immediately left and descend to the Knighton Hotel. Turn left along Broad Street, walk past the clock tower and retrace your original route back to the car.